Cross Stitch Pattern Book:

Floral Patterns - Stitching through the Seasons

Your Cross Stitch Design Patterns of Flowers and Bouquets in Spring, Summer, And Autumn

CONTENTS

CAPTURE ROMANCE OF SINGLE ROSE

Chart Size: 171 X 142 Stitches
Finished Size: 310 X 258 Mm Or 12.21 X 10.14 inch

COLORFUL TULIPS

Chart Size: 166 x 199 Stitches
Finished Size: 301 x 336 mm or 11.86 x 14.21 inch

SPRING FLOWERS

Chart Size: 112 x 109 Stitches
Finished Size: 203 x 198 mm or 8.00 x 7.79 inch

AUTUMN BOUQUET

Chart Size: 248 x 123 Stitches
Finished Size: 450 x 223 mm or 17.71 x 8.79 inch

SPRING TREBLE CLEF

Chart Size: 89 x 114 Stitches
Finished Size: 162 x 201 mm or 6.36 x 8.14 inch

INTRODUCTION

Introducing " Cross Stitch Pattern Book: Floral Patterns - Stitching through the Seasons "

Welcome to "Floral Patterns," a captivating cross stitch pattern book that invites you to embark on a melodic journey through the enchanting world of flowers and music. This book celebrates the harmonious blend of nature's beauty and the soothing melodies that resonate within our hearts.

Within these pages, you will discover a collection of five exquisite patterns, each capturing the essence of floral elegance and the magic of musical notes. From the captivating romance of a single rose to the vibrant colors of tulips, and even a delightful treble clef, these designs will ignite your creative spirit and bring joy to your stitching endeavors.

With meticulous attention to detail, each pattern has been thoughtfully crafted to ensure your stitching experience is both rewarding and enjoyable. Whether you are a seasoned cross stitch enthusiast or just beginning your stitching journey, " Floral Patterns" offers something for everyone, inviting you to explore the intersection of nature's artistry and the rhythm of music.

Immerse yourself in the splendor of each design as you create stunning embroidered masterpieces. Let the vibrant colors, intricate details, and melodic motifs transport you to a world of beauty and harmony.

As you turn the pages of this book, you will find not only the patterns themselves but also helpful tips, techniques, and guidance to enhance your stitching skills.

Discover the joy of selecting the perfect threads and creating intricate stitches that breathe life into each motif.

Whether you stitch for relaxation, self-expression, or the pure pleasure of creating something beautiful, "Floral Patterns" is your gateway to a world where art, nature, and music converge.

Let's dive into the fundamental techniques of cross stitch, as we explore the artistry of stitching on Aida 14 fabric. Begin by securing your fabric in an embroidery hoop, ensuring it's taut and ready for your creative touch. As you select your vibrant embroidery floss, keep in mind that it is usually best to separate it into 2 strands for optimal coverage and precision. Here are step-by-step guides to achieving uniform and accurate cross stitches and half stitches:

Cross stitch:

1.   Start by threading your needle with the desired number of strands of embroidery floss, usually 2 strands for Aida 14 fabric.
2.   Secure your fabric in an embroidery hoop or frame, ensuring it is taut and ready for stitching.
3.   Begin at the bottom left corner of a square on your pattern. Insert the needle from the back of the fabric, bringing it up through the bottom-left corner of the square
4.   Diagonally traverse the square, moving to the upper-right corner. Insert the needle back into the fabric at this corner, ensuring the thread lays flat across the diagonal of the square.

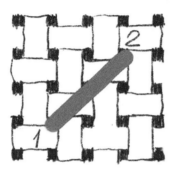

5.   From the upper-right corner, move to the upper-left corner of the square. Insert the needle into the fabric, creating a diagonal stitch that crosses over the previous stitch.
6.   Lastly, move to the lower-right corner of the square. Insert the needle into the fabric, completing the diagonal stitch and forming a perfect cross.

7.   Repeat this process, always starting from the bottom left and following the same diagonal pattern, until the desired section is complete.
8.   Keep your stitches consistent in size and tension throughout your project to achieve a uniform and professional appearance.
9.   Continue stitching row by row, following the pattern's instructions and crossing each stitch in the same direction.
10.   Take care to maintain an even tension on your stitches to prevent puckering or distortion of the fabric.
11.   As you progress, step back occasionally to admire your work and ensure that your stitches are aligned and uniform.
12.   Remember to take breaks when needed to rest your eyes and hands, as cross stitch can be a meticulous and time-consuming craft.

Half Stitch:

1. Thread your needle with the desired number of strands of embroidery floss, typically 2 strands for Aida 14 fabric.
2. Begin at the desired starting point on your pattern. Insert the needle from the back of the fabric, coming up through the bottom-left corner of a square.
3. Insert the needle back into the fabric at the top-right corner of the square, creating a diagonal stitch that covers half of the square.

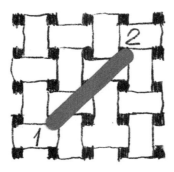

4. Pull the thread taut, but not too tight, to secure the stitch.
5. Repeat this process for each half stitch in the pattern, always working in the same direction.

To provide definition and artistic flair, master the back stitch. Bring the needle up through the fabric, a short distance away from your last stitch, and then insert it back down into the fabric, creating a straight line. Continue this process, following the pattern's outlines, as the back stitch brings structure and detail to your design. Embrace the precision of each stitch as you outline shapes, accentuate contours, and add intricate finishing touches.

In "Cross Stitch Pattern Book: Floral Patterns - Stitching through the Seasons," all the design patterns are specifically created for Aida 14 fabric. Aida 14 is a popular choice among cross stitchers, as it provides a balanced stitching experience. With 14 crosses per inch, each stitch fits neatly within a square, allowing for precise and consistent results. The fabric's weave structure makes it easy to count and follow the pattern. When working on the patterns in this book, remember to use Aida 14 fabric for the best stitch coverage and design compatibility. As a general guideline, be sure to add at least 3 inches (7.6 centimeters) of extra fabric on each side of the design to allow for framing and finishing.

By following these steps and maintaining a consistent approach to your cross stitches, you will create a stunning and uniform design that showcases the beauty of the blooming flowers in your "Floral Patterns" project. Enjoy the journey of each stitch as you bring your floral masterpiece to life!

In order to provide you with the utmost convenience and flexibility, we have ensured that all patterns in this book are available in both color and black-and-white variants. We understand that every stitcher has their own preferences and stitching style, so we wanted to cater to your individual needs. Additionally, for patterns that include backstitch, we have included four different versions: color pattern with backstitch, color pattern without backstitch, black and white pattern with backstitch, and black and white pattern without backstitch. This allows you to choose the style that suits you best and ensures that you have all the options at your disposal to bring these beautiful floral designs to life. Happy stitching!

THE MAGIC OF A SINGLE ROSE

Overview
Palette: DMC
Colors: 36+6 blends
Stitches used: full cross stitch
Fabric: 14 Aida White
Chart Size: 171 x 142 Stitches
Finished Size: 310 x 258 mm or 12.21 x 10.14 inch

The Enchanting Beauty of a Single Rose:
A Captivating Cross-Stitch Design

Prepare to embark on an extraordinary cross-stitch adventure with the enchanting "Capture Romance of Single Rose" pattern. This design breaks free from the ordinary, surpassing the boundaries of size and depth to offer you a stitching experience like no other. Get ready to bring a rose to life with every meticulous stitch!

The allure of this pattern lies in its elegant simplicity. Though it may appear large, measuring 310 x 258 mm or 12.21 x 10.14 inches, it allows you to create a stunning three-dimensional effect. With just 36 colors and 6 blends, you'll unlock the intricate beauty of this exquisite rose, all without the need for any backstitching.

As you work through the embroidery, watch in awe as the rose petals gracefully emerge from the frame, capturing your gaze with their delicate charm. The original design showcases dark green leaves as a backdrop, perfectly accentuating the richness of the pink hues adorning each petal. However, for those who appreciate minimalism, the background can be omitted.

Embarking on the "Capture Romance of Single Rose" pattern is an invitation to immerse yourself in the timeless magic of nature's wonders. Let your needle and thread become the tools for expressing the enchantment and romance that this beloved flower represents. With each stitch, you'll weave a work of art that encapsulates the essence of love and passion. Get ready to embark on a stitching journey filled with boundless creativity and joy!

Thread Length Table (DMC # / Length, meters)

DMC 23 - 6,94	DMC 316 - 1,91	DMC 963 - 1,49	DMC 3722 - 0,47
DMC 33 - 15,4	DMC 367 - 11,28	DMC 986 - 1,61	DMC 3726 - 0,24
DMC 34 - 0,57	DMC 554 - 2,09	DMC 3350 - 23,91	DMC 3727 - 6,43
DMC 35 - 0,34	DMC 604 - 17,61	DMC 3354 - 4,4	DMC 3731 - 0,72
DMC 150 - 5,16	DMC 605 - 7,97	DMC 3363 - 2,07	DMC 3772 - 1,27
DMC 151 - 1,61	DMC 640 - 1,22	DMC 3608 - 4,22	DMC 3779 - 1,66
DMC 153 - 31,81	DMC 758 - 0,06	DMC 3609 - 8,83	DMC 3802 - 3,79
DMC 154 - 5,32	DMC 777 - 1,47	DMC 3685 - 2,35	DMC 3803 - 10,85
DMC 209 - 19,93	DMC 814 - 4,77	DMC 3687 - 26,05	DMC 3806 - 9,12
DMC 211 - 4,91	DMC 815 - 20,29	DMC 3688 - 10	DMC 3833 - 0,94
DMC 310 - 4,27	DMC 818 - 3,33	DMC 3689 - 4,32	DMC 3834 - 0,8
DMC 315 - 0,39	DMC 890 - 22,5	DMC 3712 - 0,18	DMC 3835 - 1,3
			DMC 3860 - 0,34

Instructions and Symbol Key for Design "Romance of Single Rose"

Fabric: 14 count

Stitches: 171 x 142   **Size:** 12.21 x 10.14 inches or 31.02 x 25.76 cm

Colours: DMC

Use **2** strands of thread for cross stitch

Sym	No.	Sym	No.
	23		33
	34		35
	150		151
	153		154
	209		211
	310		315
	316		367
	554		604
	605		640
	758		777
	814		815
	818		890
	963		986
	3350		3354
	3363		3608
	3609		3685
	3687		3688
	3689		3712
	3722		3726
	3727		3731
	3772		3779
	3802		3803
	3806		3833
	3834		3835
	3860		209 + 33
	3806 + 604		604 + 605
	3687 + 3688		3688 + 3689

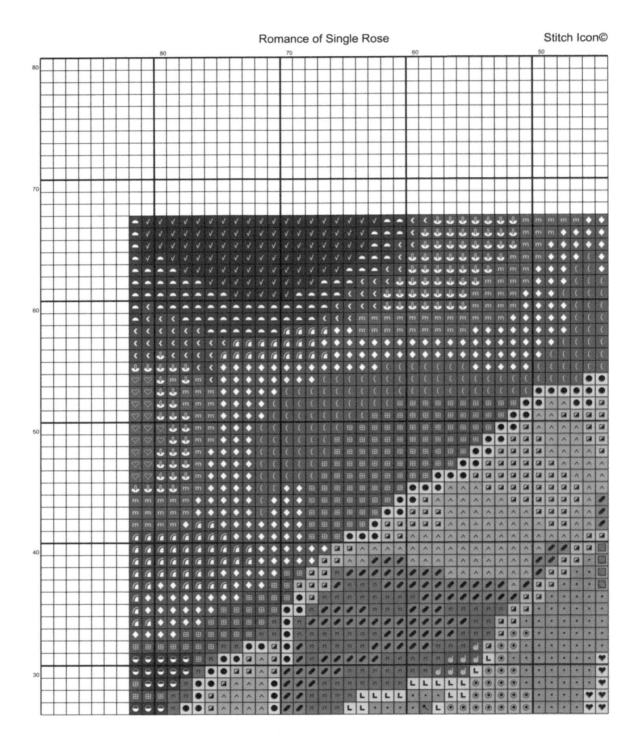

Stitch Icon©

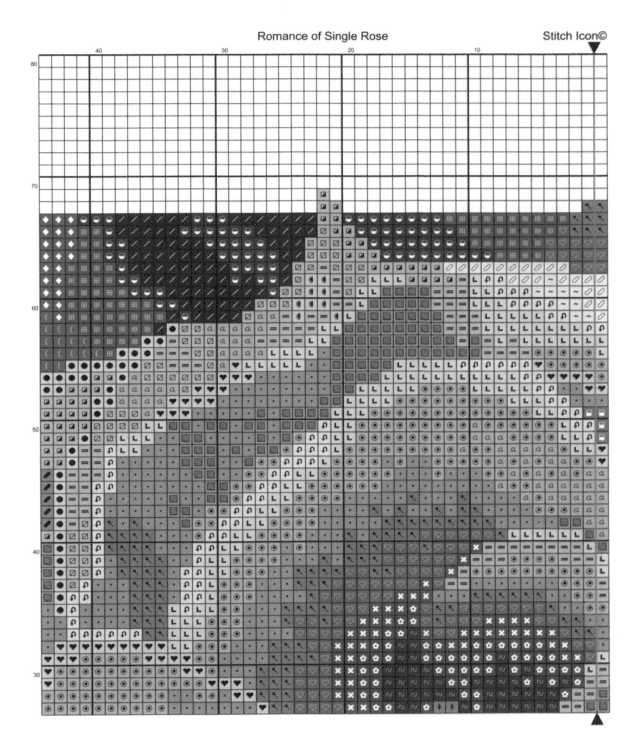

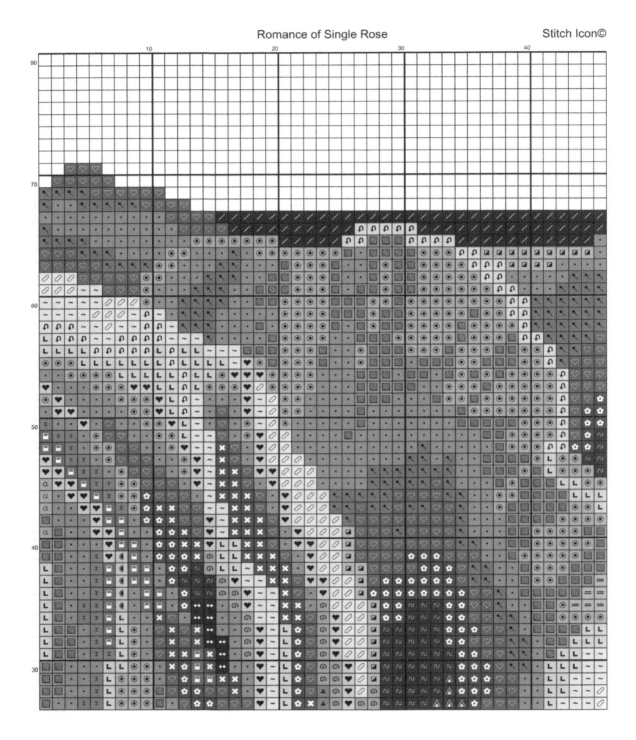

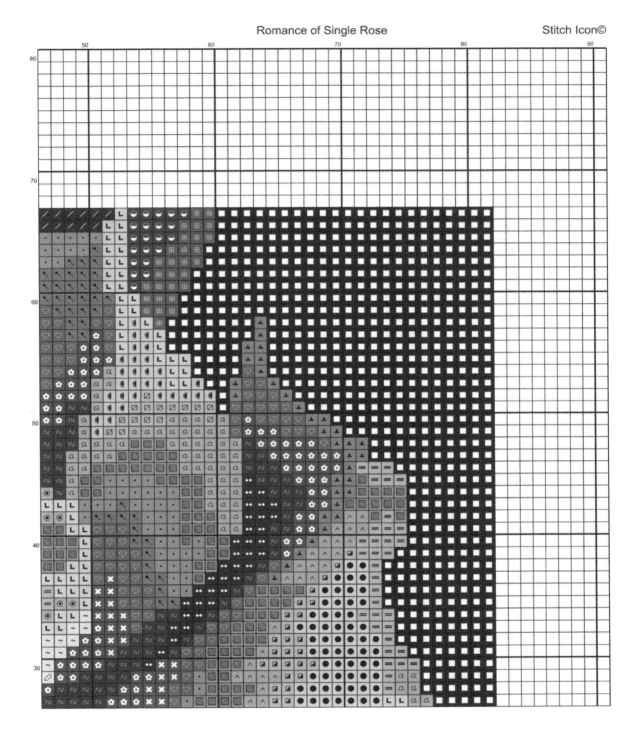

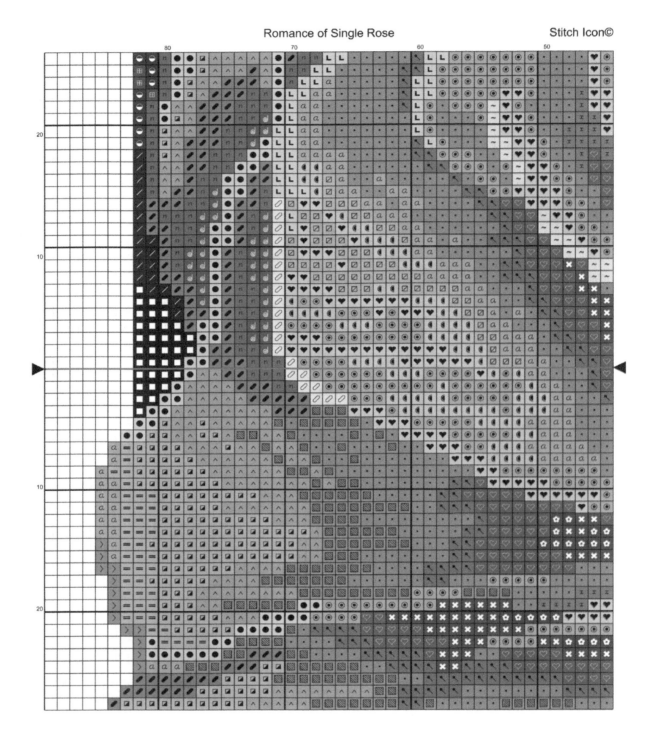

Romance of Single Rose

Stitch Icon©

Stitch Icon©

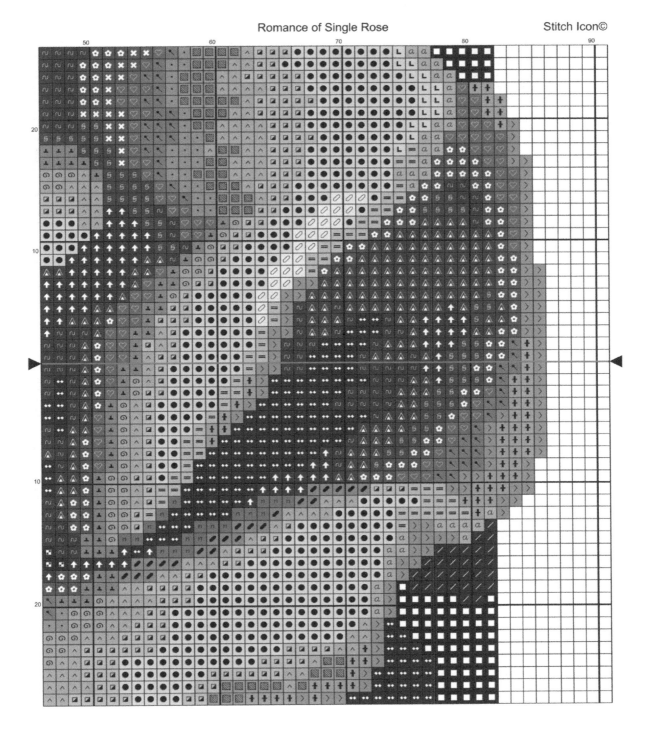

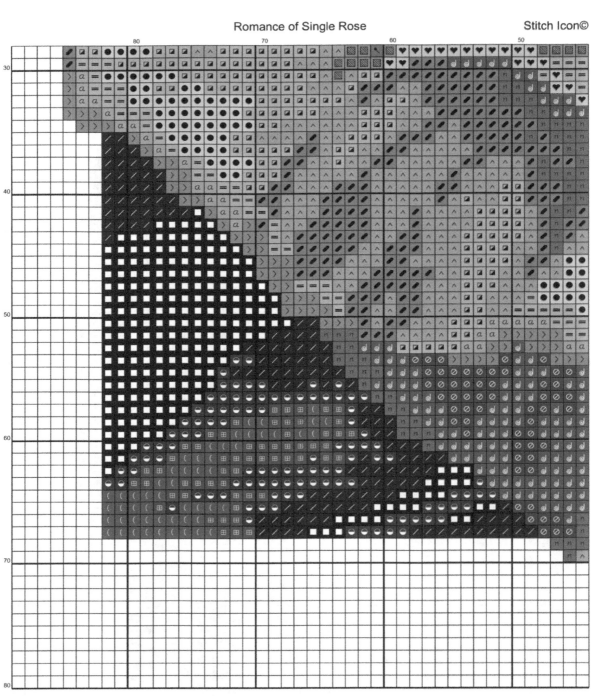

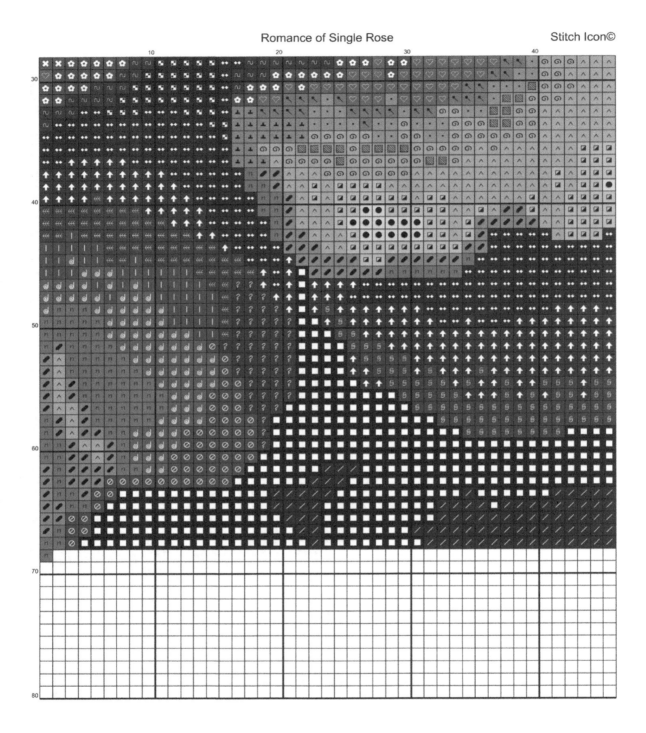

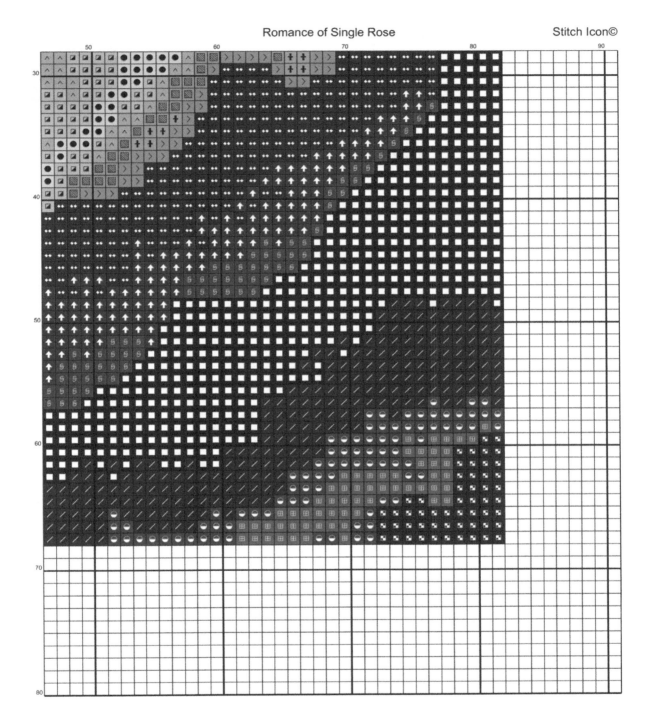

Instructions and Symbol Key for Design "Romance of Single Rose"

Fabric: **14** count

Stitches: 171 x 142   **Size:** 12.21 x 10.14 inches or 31.02 x 25.76 cm

Colours: DMC

Use **2** strands of thread for cross stitch

Sym	No.	Sym	No.
⊘	23	♂	33
I	34	⧱	35
✿	150	♥	151
▨	153	▧	154
✎	209	●	211
■	310	▬	315
⊥	316	⊞	367
∧	554	α	604
◖	605	◆	640
▶	758	⚠	777
↔	814	℧	815
~	818	/	890
∩	963	◒	986
✖	3350	◉	3354
(	3363	▨	3608
=	3609	↑	3685
♡	3687	·	3688
L	3689	‡	3712
⚓	3722	‹	3726
℧	3727	▣	3731
m	3772	◎	3779
√	3802	ʂ	3803
⟩	3806	ɪ	3833
?	3834	⊘	3835
◖	3860	n	209 + 33
†	3806 + 604	▨	604 + 605
⟍	3687 + 3688	2	3688 + 3689

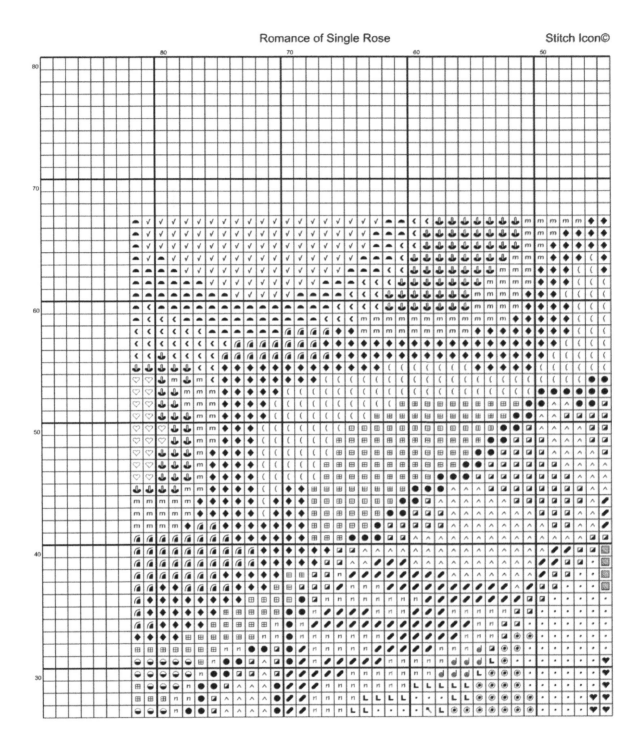

Stitch Icon©

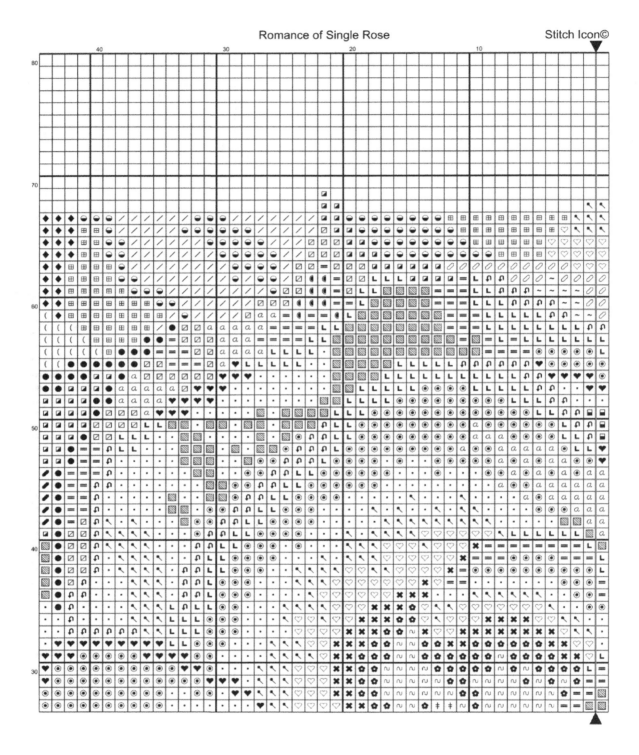

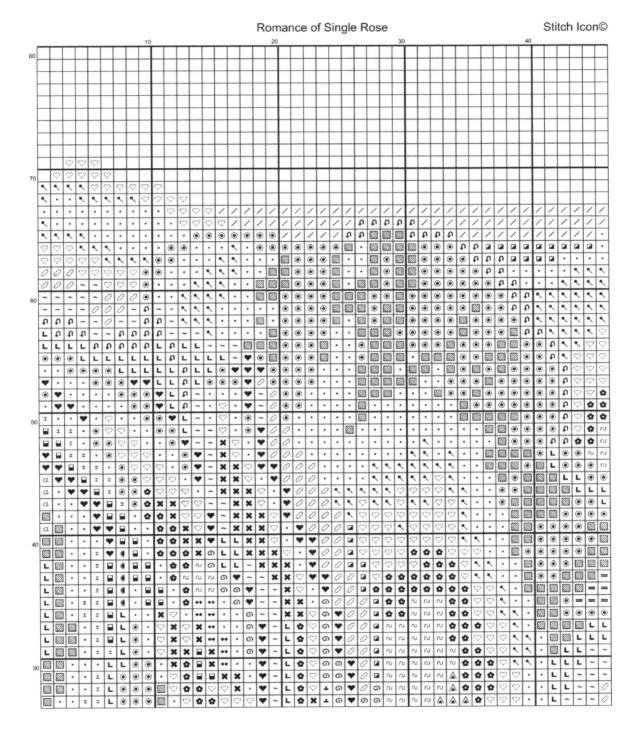

Romance of Single Rose

Stitch Icon©

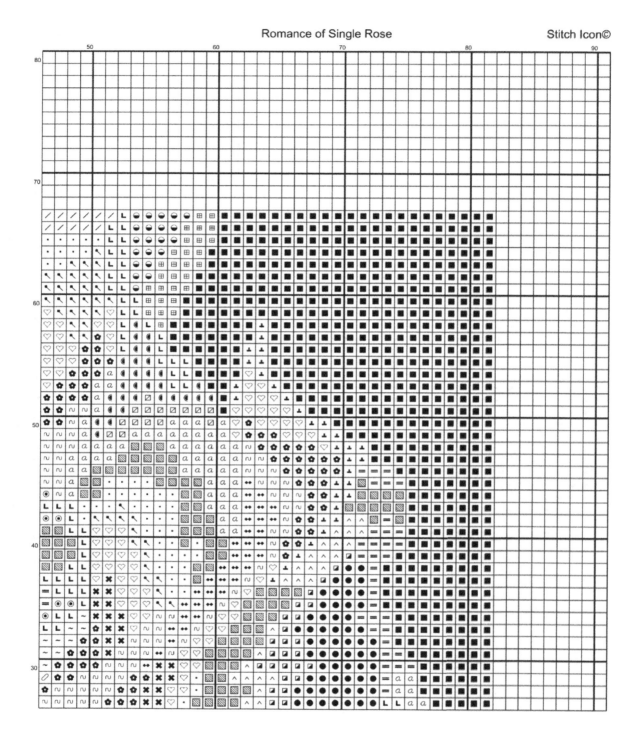

Stitch Icon©

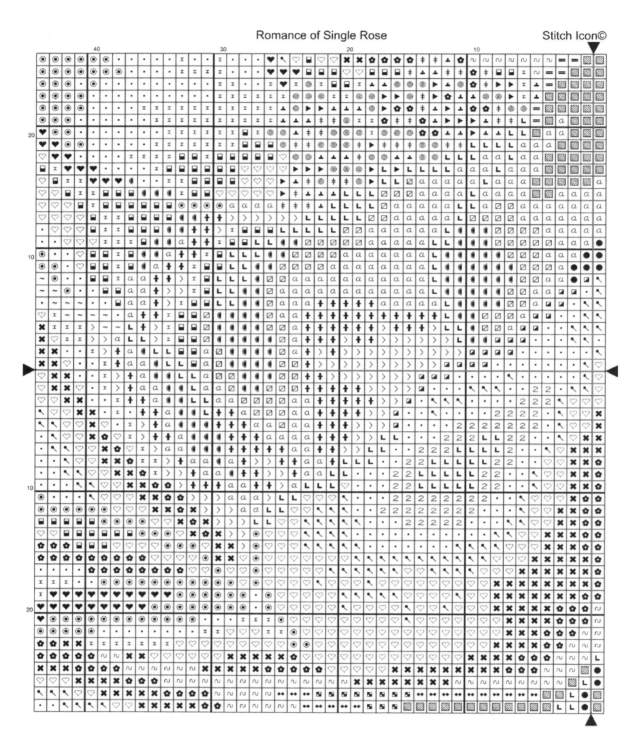

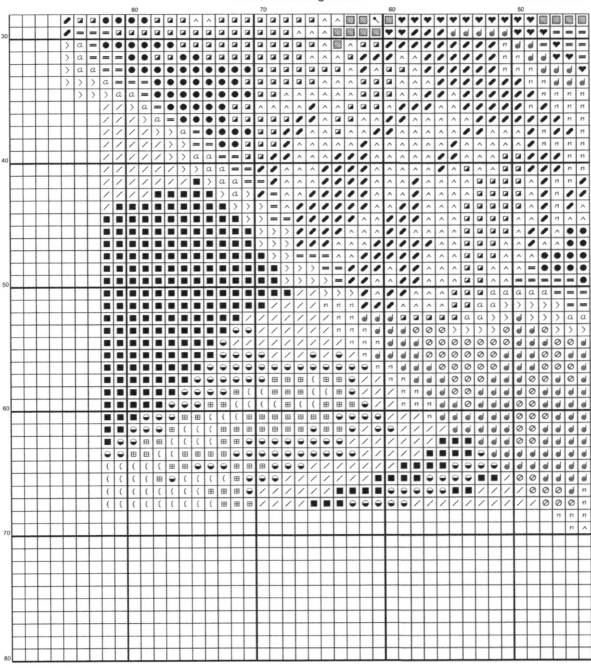

Stitch Icon©

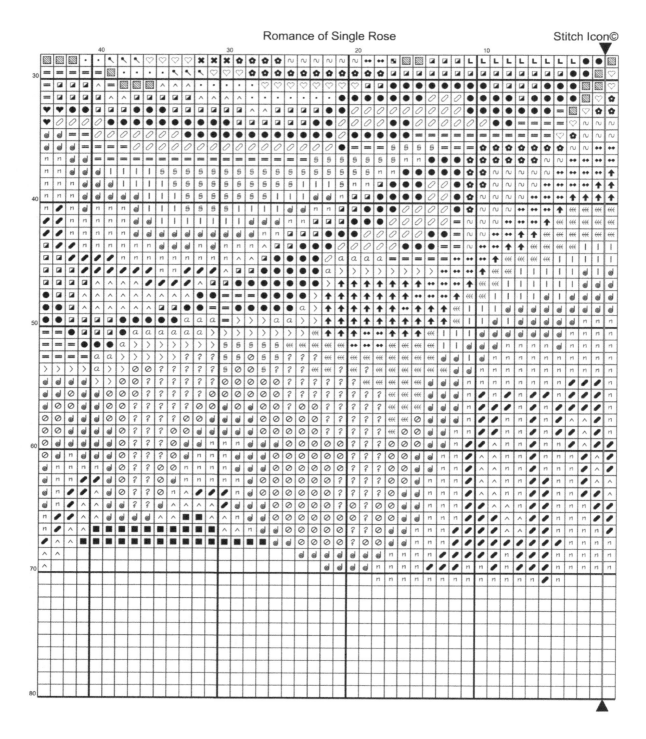

COLORFUL TULIPS

<u>Overview</u>

Palette: DMC
Colors: 58 + 2 blends
Stitches used: full cross stitch, backstitch
Fabric: 14 Aida
Chart Size: 166 x 199 Stitches
Finished Size: 301 x 336 mm or 11.86 x 14.21 inch

35

Unveiling Beauty: The Colorful Tulips Cross-Stitch Masterpiece

Prepare to be enchanted by the mesmerizing beauty of the "Colorful Tulips" composition. In this exquisite design, a delightful bouquet of tulips takes center stage, nestled in an old teapot that adds a touch of nostalgia and charm. Despite its simplicity, this arrangement captures the essence of a cozy home filled with warmth and love.

The cross-stitch designer has meticulously chosen 58 shades of pink, green, and gray to bring the elements to life. Each tulip, with its vibrant stem and leaves, radiates a lively spirit that is both captivating and realistic. The teapot, expertly rendered with shades of gray, exudes an air of timeless elegance.

Amidst this symphony of colors, a lone blue ribbon serves as a gentle reminder that love finds a place even in the absence of a traditional vase. With a modest embroidery size of 301 x 336 mm or 11.86 x 14.21 inches, this design offers a canvas for creativity that transcends mere craftsmanship.

With every stitch, you breathe life into the fabric, infusing it with meaning and capturing the magic of this captivating still life. Embrace the delicate petals of each tulip, the graceful curves of the teapot, and the harmonious interplay of colors that weave together to create a masterpiece worthy of admiration. Let your needle be your brush, painting a portrait of love, warmth, and the timeless beauty found in nature's precious gifts.

Thread Length Table (DMC # / Length, meters)

DMC 3 - 9,48	DMC 368 - 3,26	DMC 818 - 6,2	DMC 3350 - 2,51
DMC 10 - 0,68	DMC 369 - 0,28	DMC 917 - 0,23	DMC 3607 - 1,71
DMC 15 - 0,06	DMC 372 - 0,97	DMC 931 - 10,54	DMC 3608 - 23,16
DMC 23 - 5,33	DMC 415 - 23,4	DMC 932 - 8,71	DMC 3609 - 12,24
DMC 34 - 2,69	DMC 552 - 0,99	DMC 961 - 0,23	DMC 3687 - 0,51
DMC 35 - 0,18	DMC 553 - 0,23	DMC 966 - 12,37	DMC 3688 - 6,72
DMC 151 - 19,66	DMC 554 - 0,87	DMC 986 - 2,57	DMC 3727 - 9,73
DMC 153 - 13,7	DMC 601 - 0,6	DMC 987 - 1,25	DMC 3805 - 0,61
DMC 157 - 0,57	DMC 604 - 1	DMC 989 - 20,56	DMC 3806 - 21,05
DMC 209 - 5,48	DMC 605 - 3,81	DMC 3023 - 3,53	DMC 3832 - 1,48
DMC 211 - 4,49	DMC 611 - 0,22	DMC 3024 - 0,25	DMC 3836 - 0,22
DMC 309 - 0,4	DMC 642 - 1,3	DMC 3046 - 0,62	DMC 3865 - 24,19
DMC 310 - 27,95	DMC 718 - 12,12	DMC 3047 - 0,77	DMC 3866 - 3,62
DMC 316 - 0,49	DMC 762 - 7,83	DMC 3326 - 0,19	
DMC 320 - 1,23	DMC 775 - 5,14	DMC 3348 - 3,84	

Instructions and Symbol Key for Design "Colorful Tulips"

Fabric: 14 count White Aida

Stitches: 166 x 199   **Size:**   11.86 x 14.21 inches or 30.12 x 36.10 cm

Colours: DMC

Use **2** strands of thread for cross stitch

Sym	No.	Sym	No.
~	3		10
♣	15	%	23
	34		35
◖	151	♡	153
▲	157	●	209
#	211	□	309
⚓	310	⧓	316
♥	320	◩	368
✗	369	◉	372
↻	415	Z	552
–	553	↘	554
L	601	=	604
e	605	◄►	611
←	642	◆	718
↘	762	◗	775
⋘	818	I	917
▫	931	S	932
⌗	961	c	966
U	986	▣	987
?	989	n	3023
◈	3024	▲	3046
V	3047	△	3326
T	3348	◖	3350
∅	3607	∧	3608
@	3609	✕	3687
▨	3688	ᴎ	3727
		3805	⚓	3806
⚲	3832	✿	3836
·	3865	✚	3866
◤	415 + 762	(	3865 + 762

Backstitch

Use **1** strand of thread for backstitch

————————   DMC 310

————————   DMC 3865

Use 2 strands of thread for backstitch

————————   DMC 310

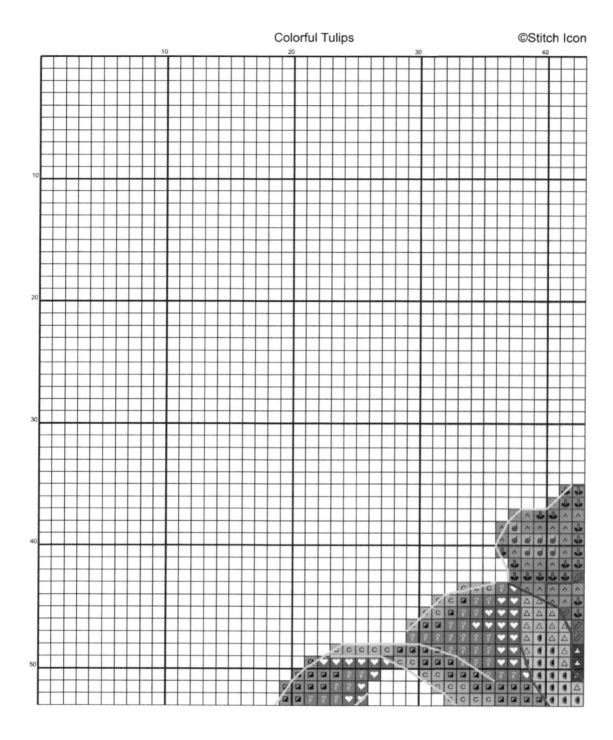

Colorful Tulips

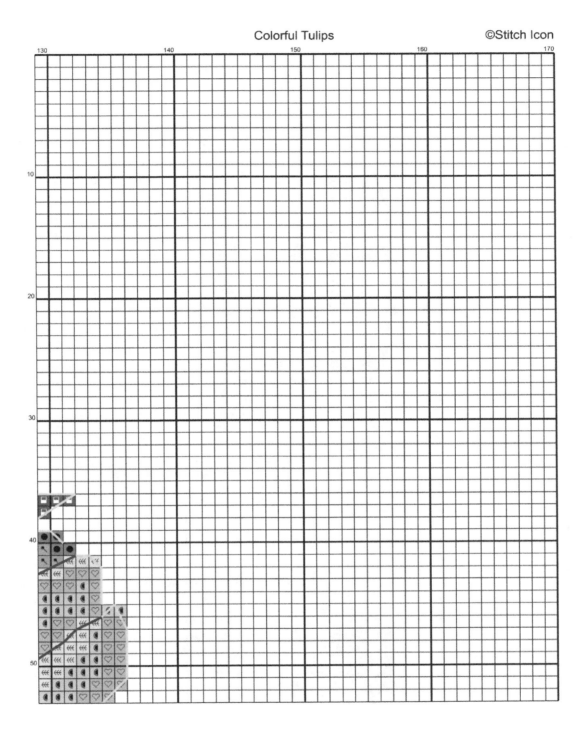

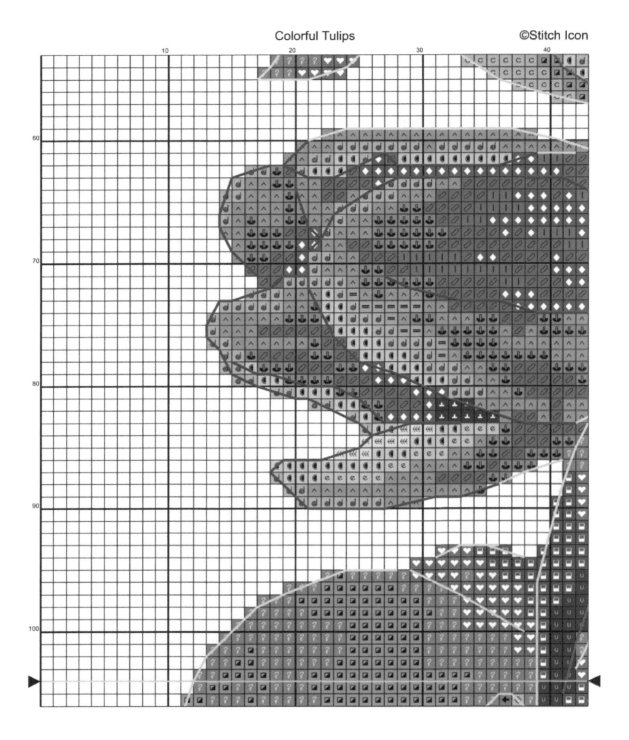

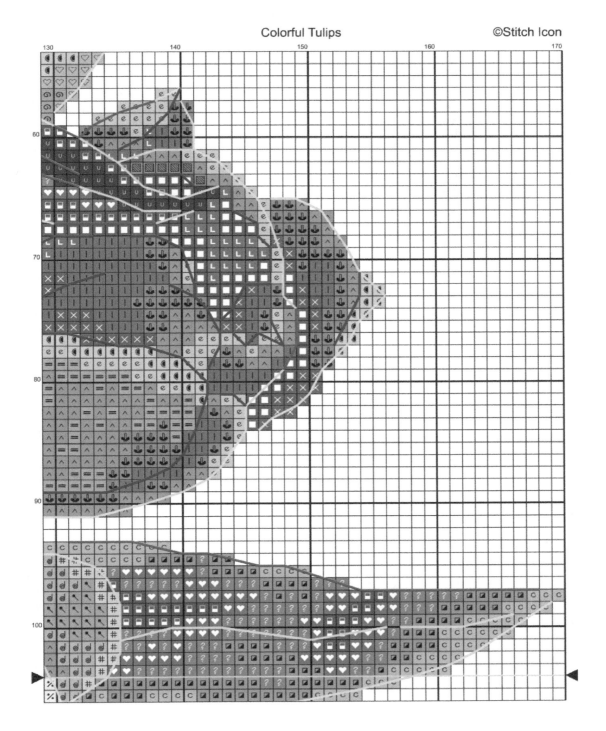

Colorful Tulips ©Stitch Icon

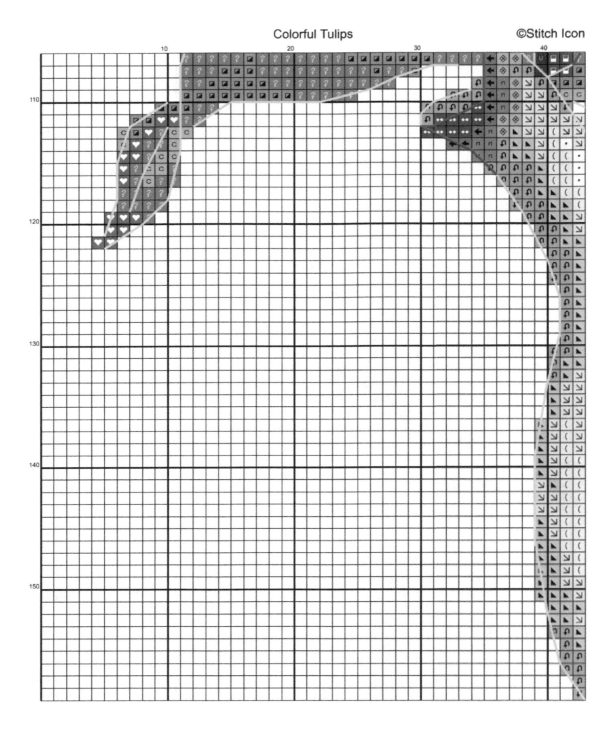

46

Colorful Tulips ©Stitch Icon

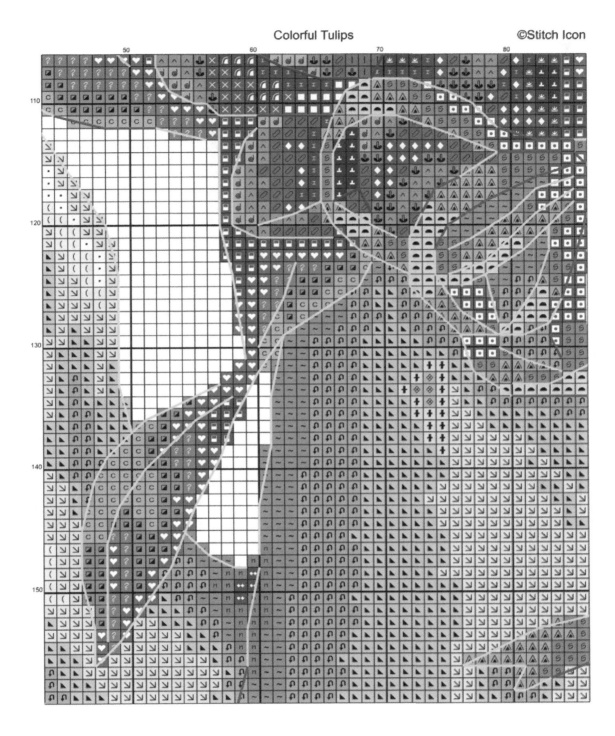

47

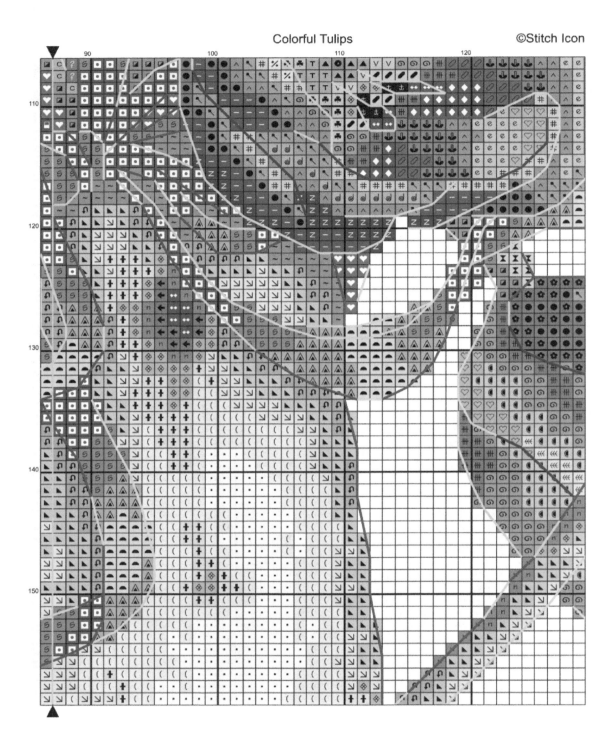

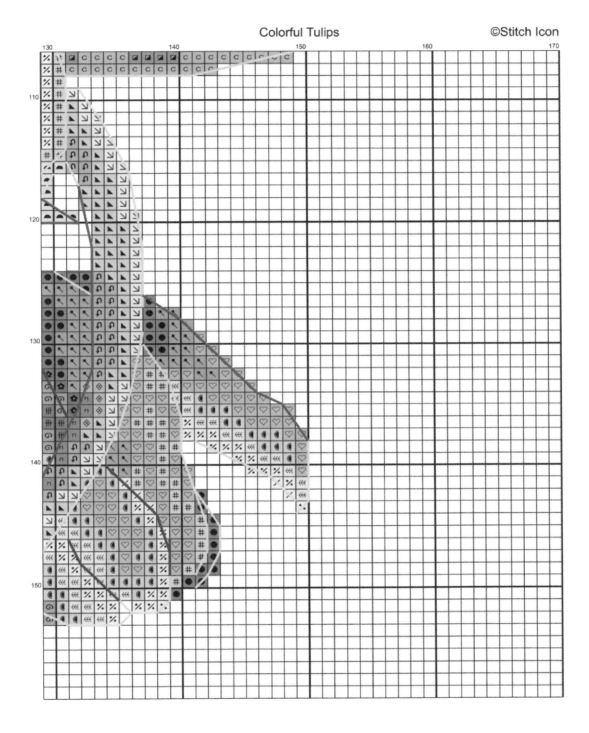

Colorful Tulips

©Stitch Icon

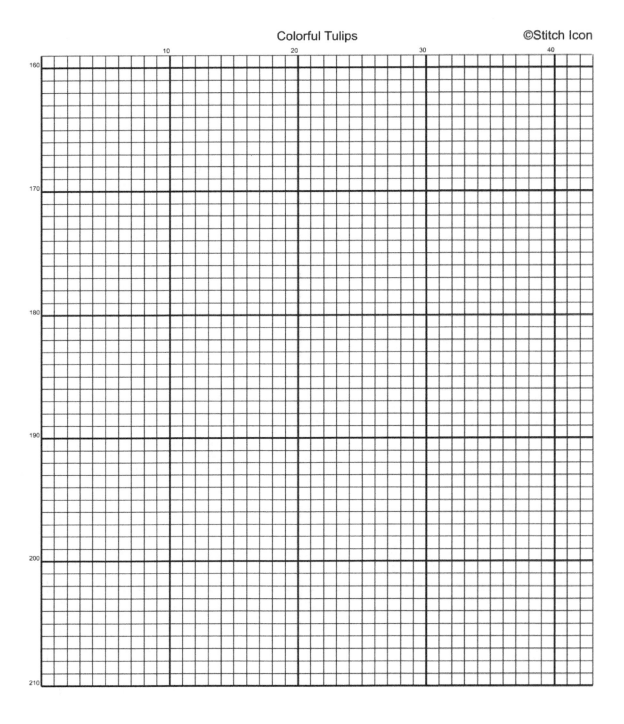

Colorful Tulips

©Stitch Icon

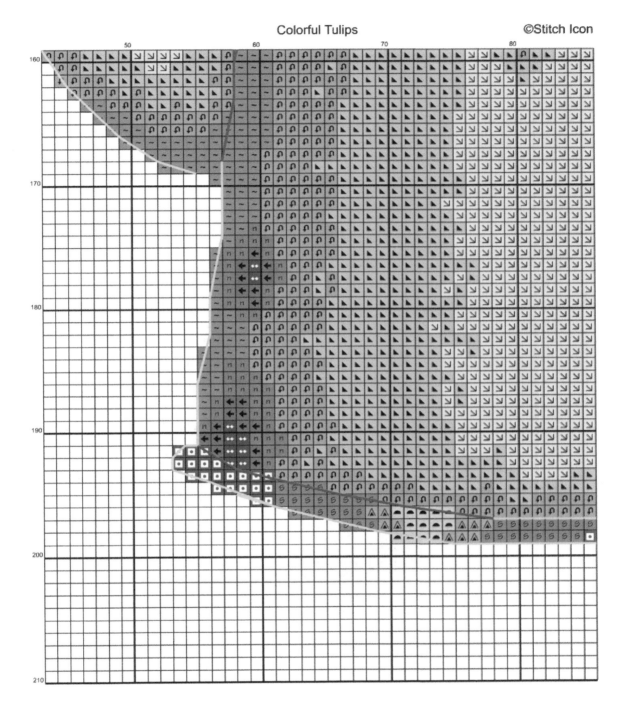

51

Colorful Tulips ©Stitch Icon

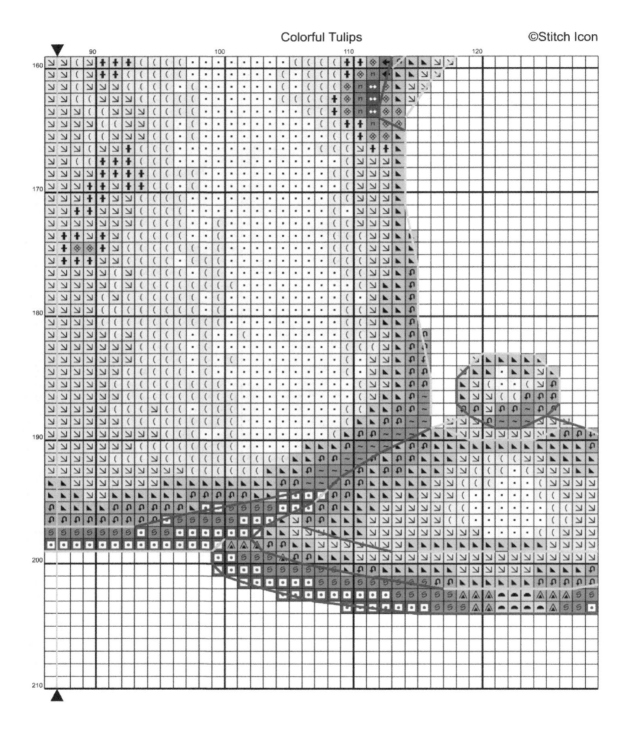

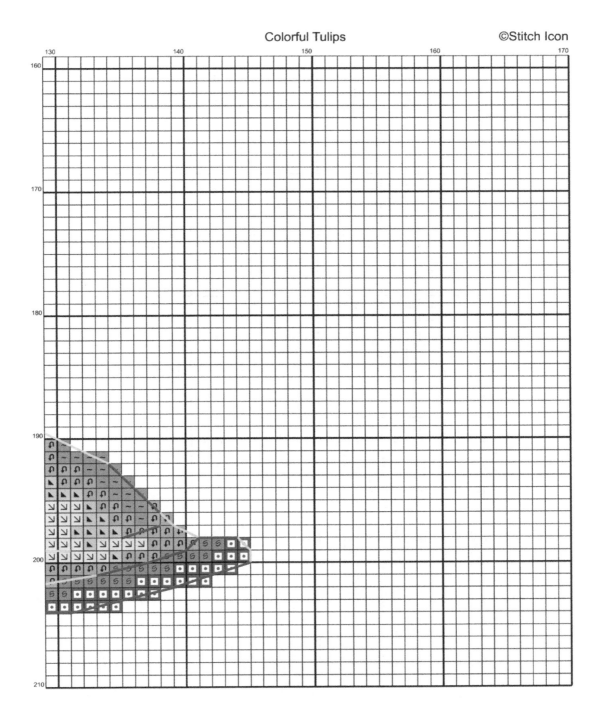

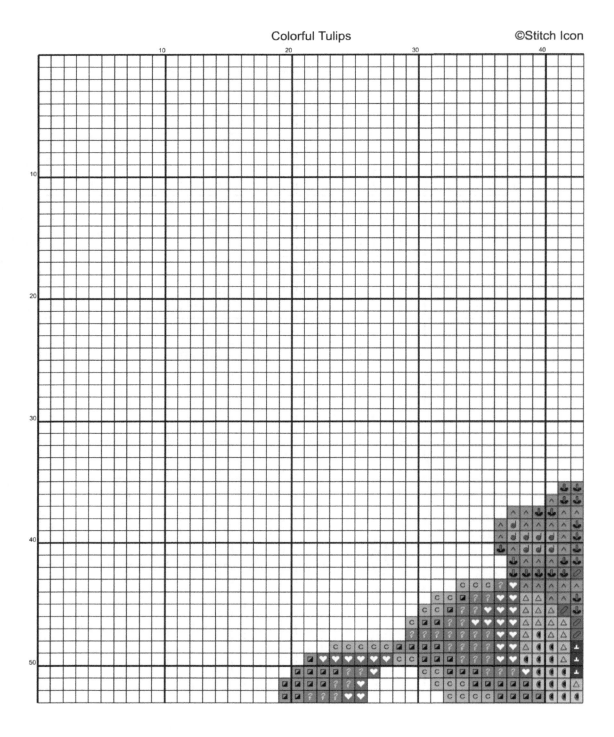

Colorful Tulips
©Stitch Icon

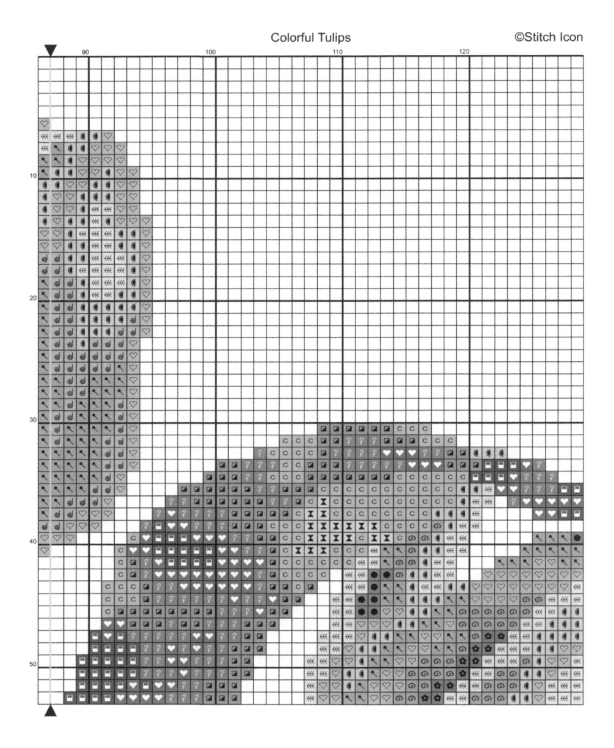

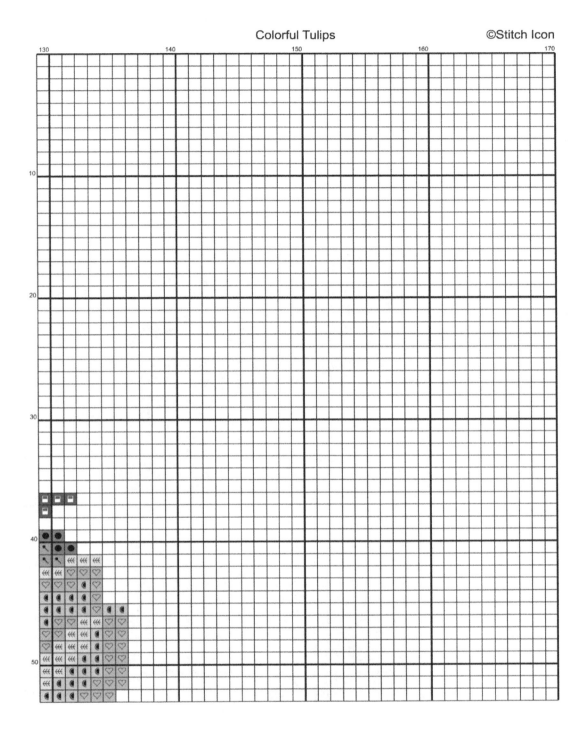

©Stitch Icon

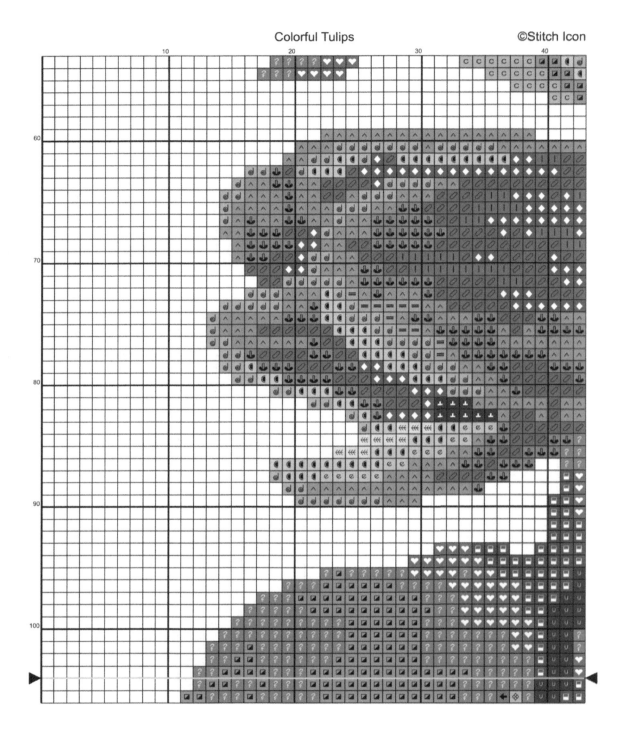

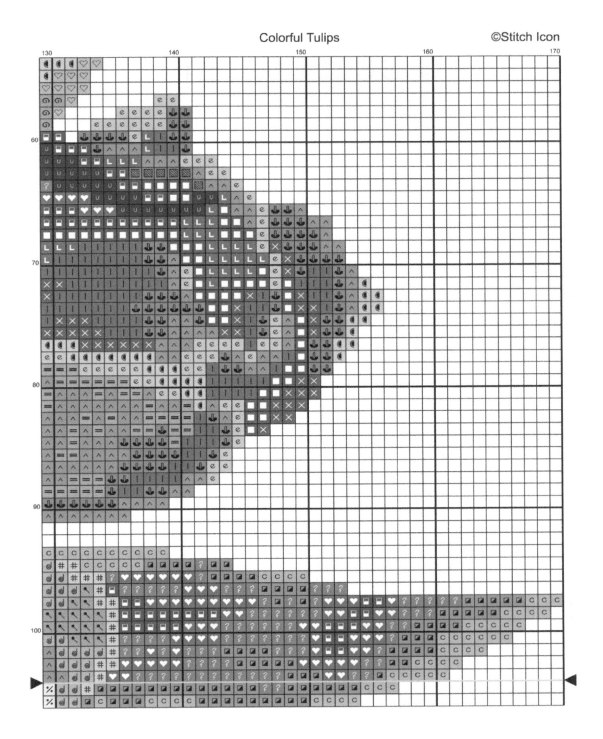

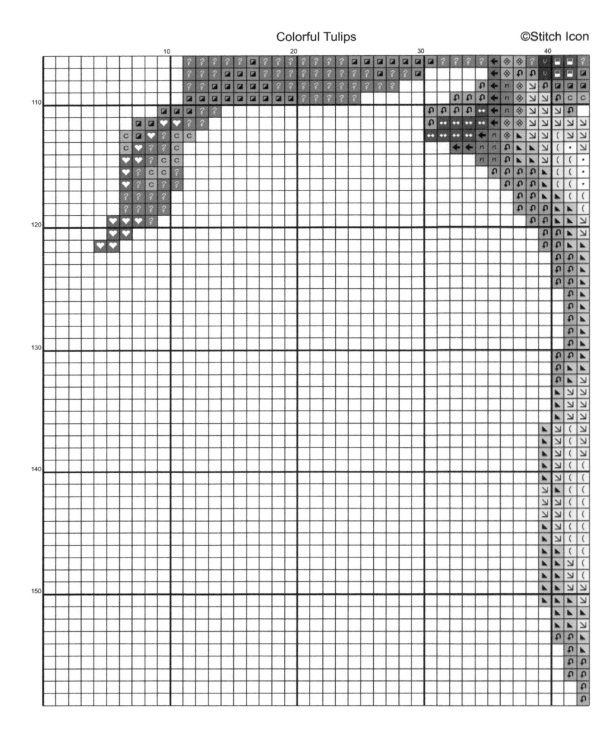

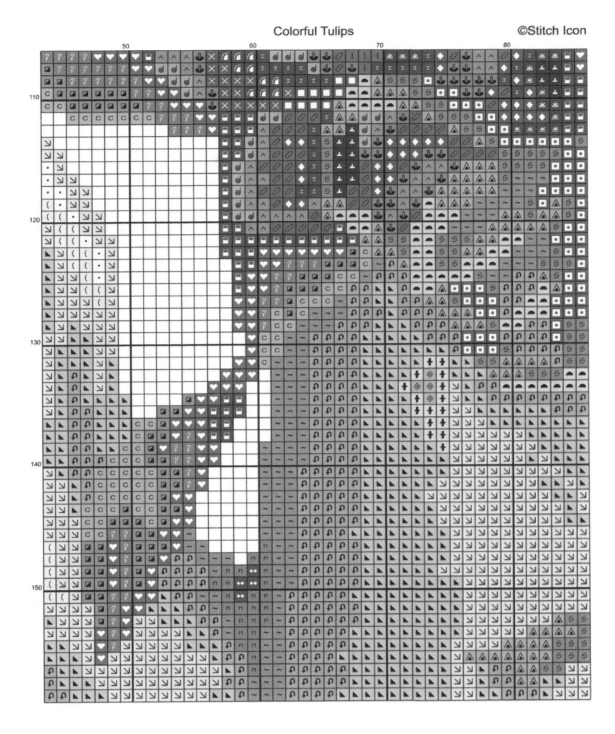

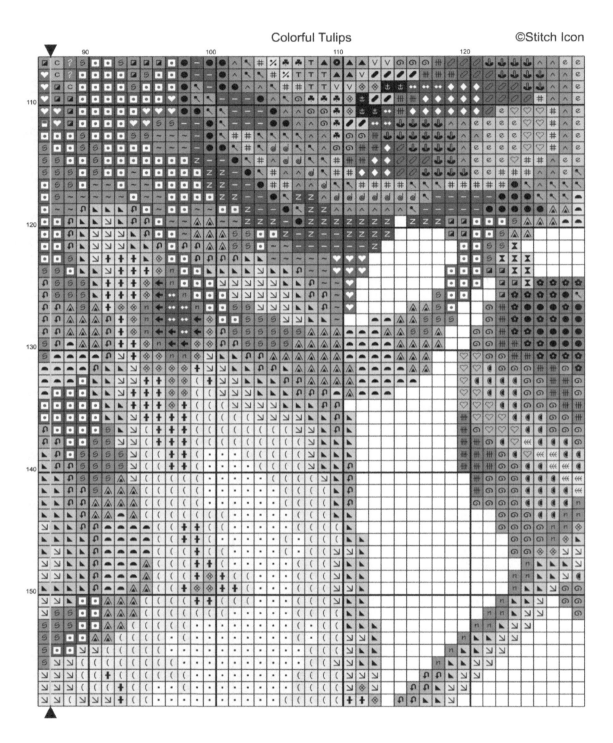

Colorful Tulips

©Stitch Icon

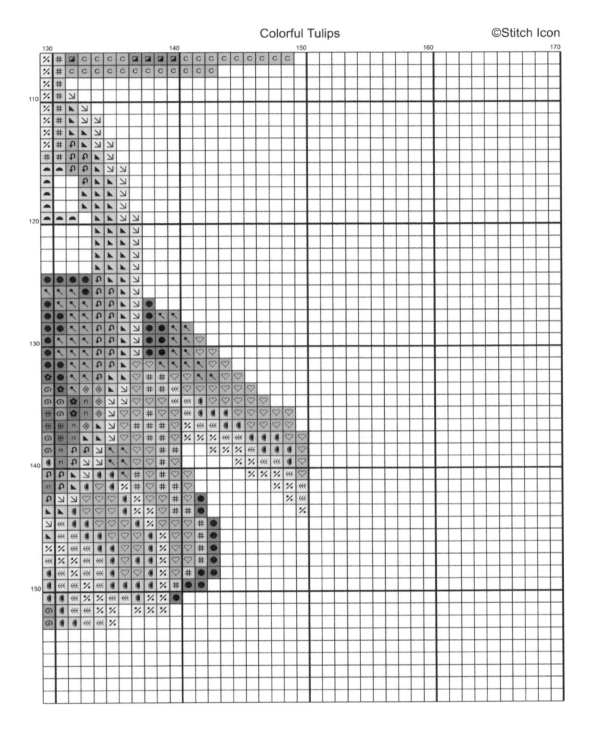

65

Colorful Tulips

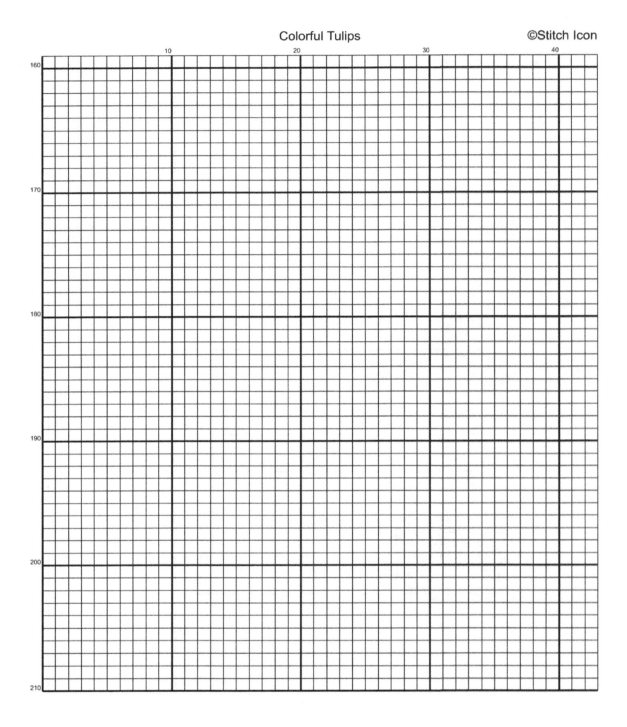

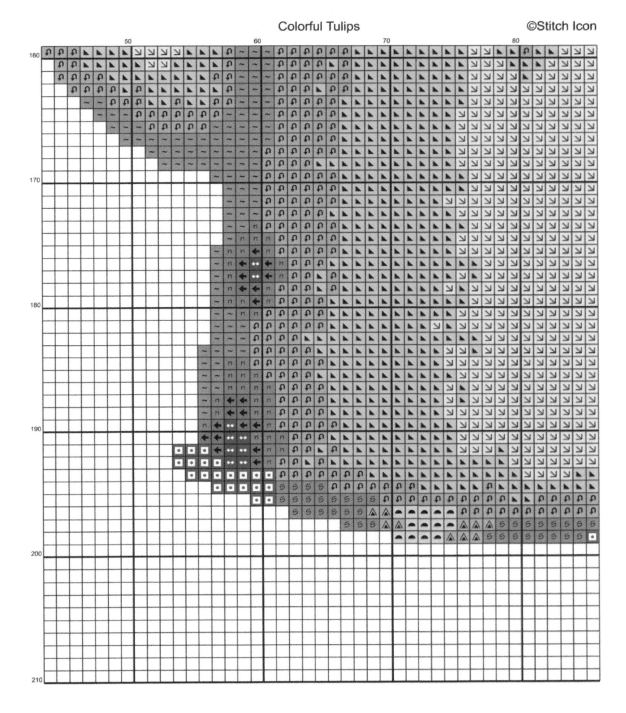

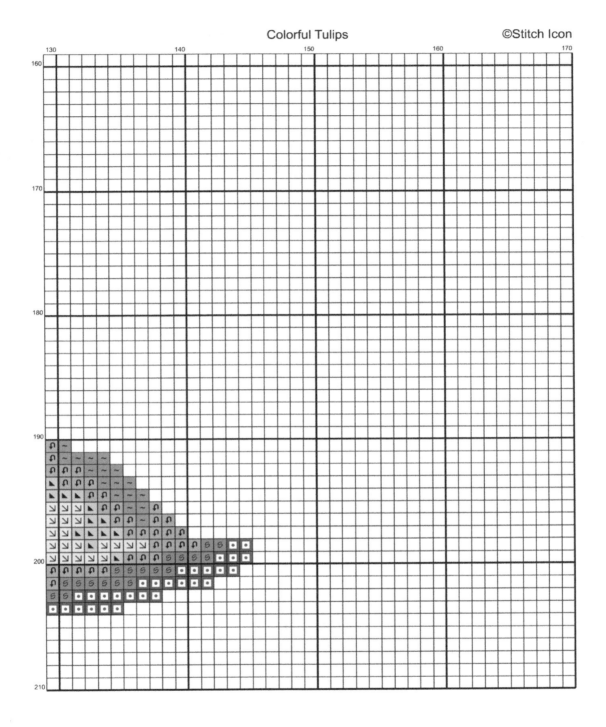

Instructions and Symbol Key for Design "Colorful Tulips"

Fabric: **14** count White Aida

Stitches: 166 x 199   **Size:**   11.86 x 14.21 inches or 30.12 x 36.10 cm

Colours: DMC

Use **2** strands of thread for cross stitch

Sym	No.		Sym	No.
~	3		✎	10
♣	15		✂	23
✹	34		⊥	35
◖	151		♡	153
⚠	157		●	209
#	211		■	309
‡	310		⧻	316
♥	320		◪	368
✖	369		◉	372
⌂	415		z	552
–	553		➚	554
L	601		=	604
e	605		◆◆	611
←	642		◆	718
↘	762		◣	775
⋘	818		ɪ	917
◘	931		ꜱ	932
⊞	961		c	966
∪	986		⧠	987
?	989		n	3023
⊗	3024		▲	3046
V	3047		△	3326
T	3348		◪	3350
∅	3607		∧	3608
◉	3609		×	3687
▨	3688		၍	3727
I	3805		⚓	3806
♪	3832		✿	3836
•	3865		✝	3866
◤	415 + 762		(	3865 + 762

Backstitch

Use **1** strand of thread for backstitch

————————————   DMC 310

————————————   DMC 3865

Use **2** strands of thread for backstitch

————————————   DMC 310

Colorful Tulips   ©Stitch Icon

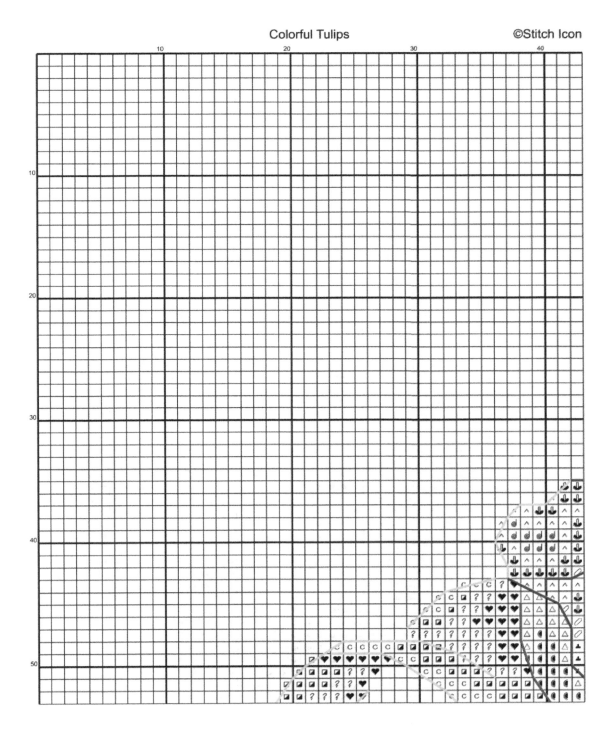

71

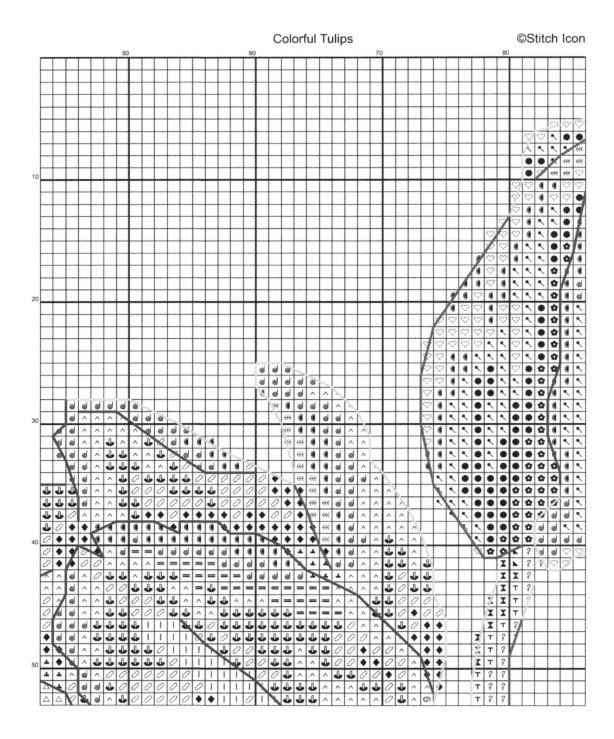

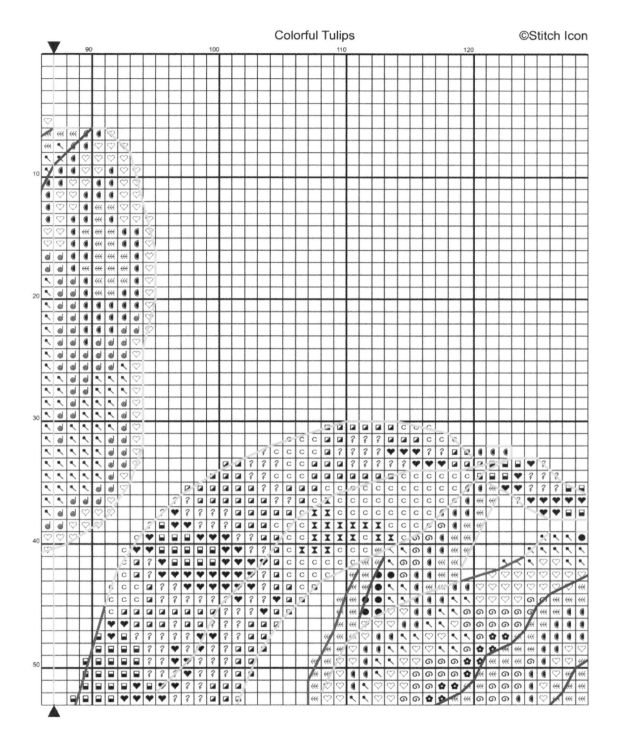

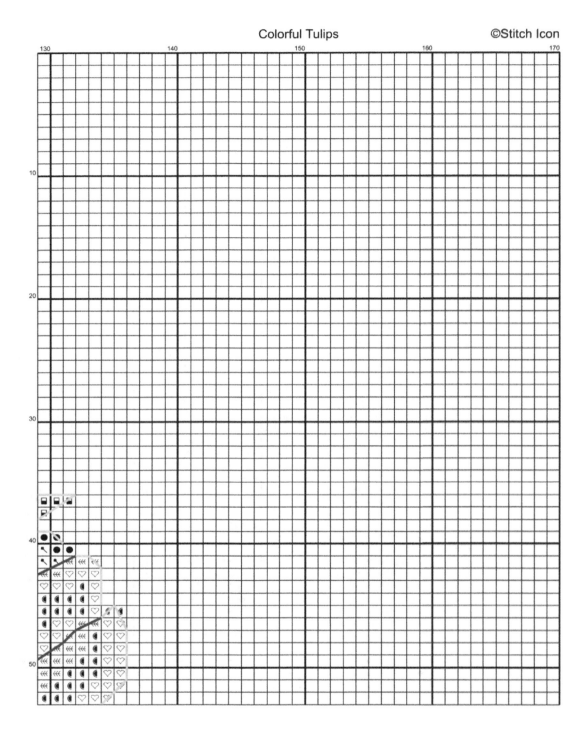

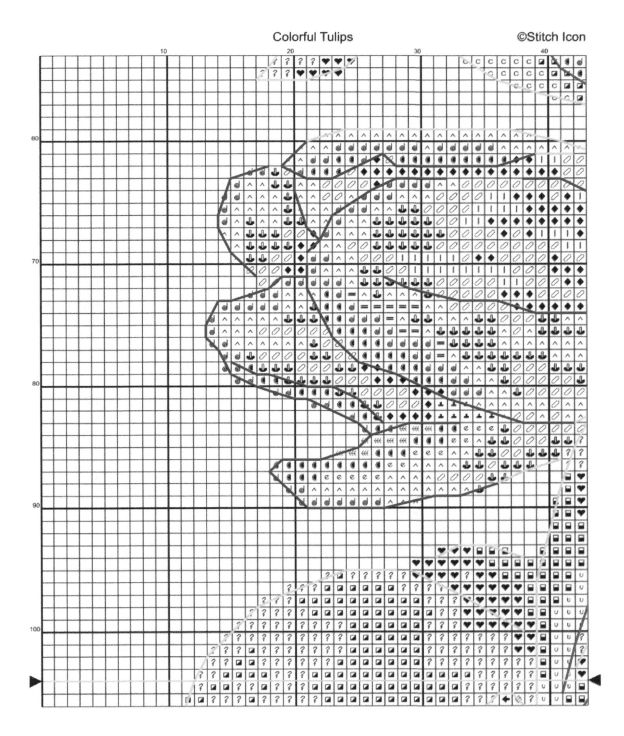

Colorful Tulips ©Stitch Icon

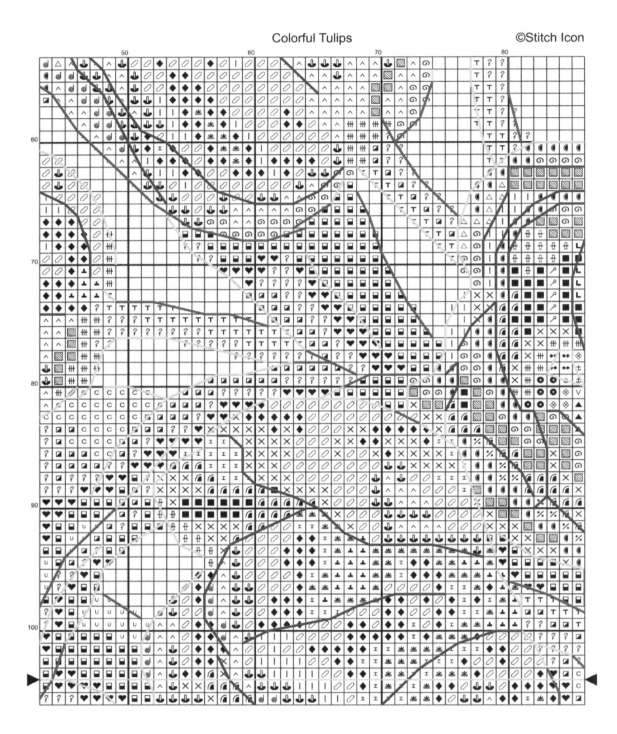

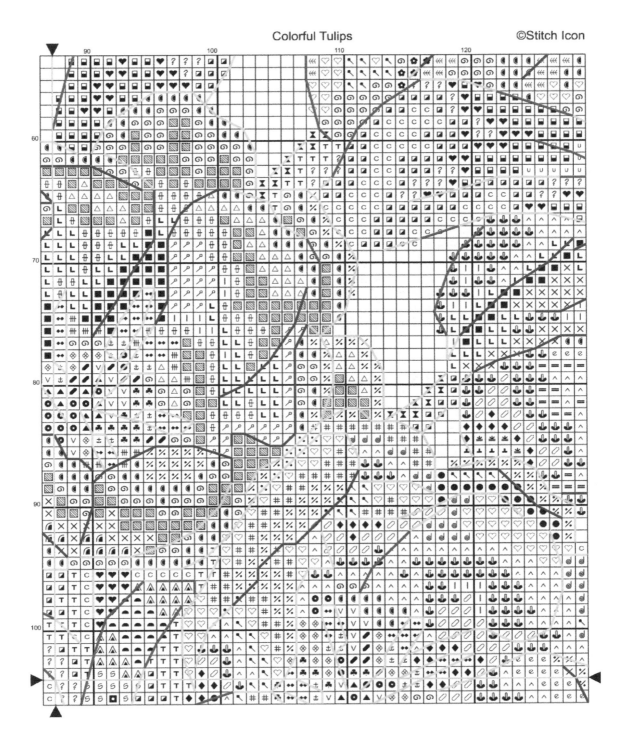

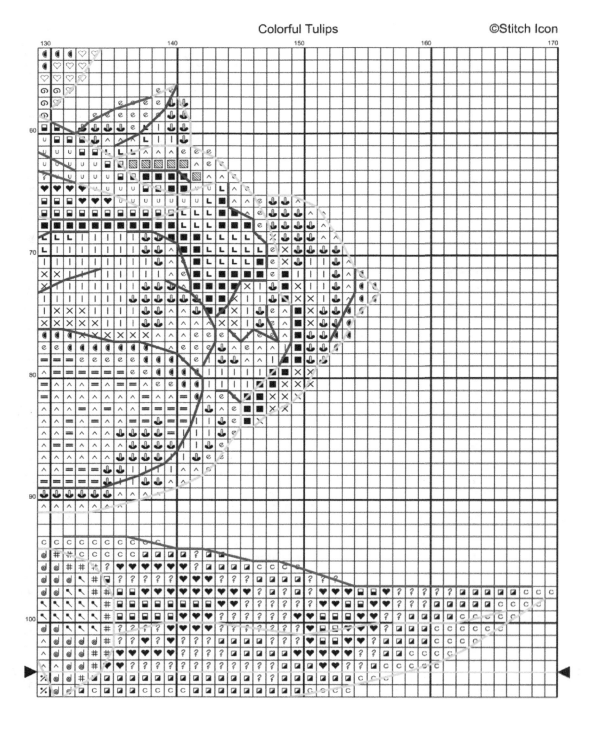

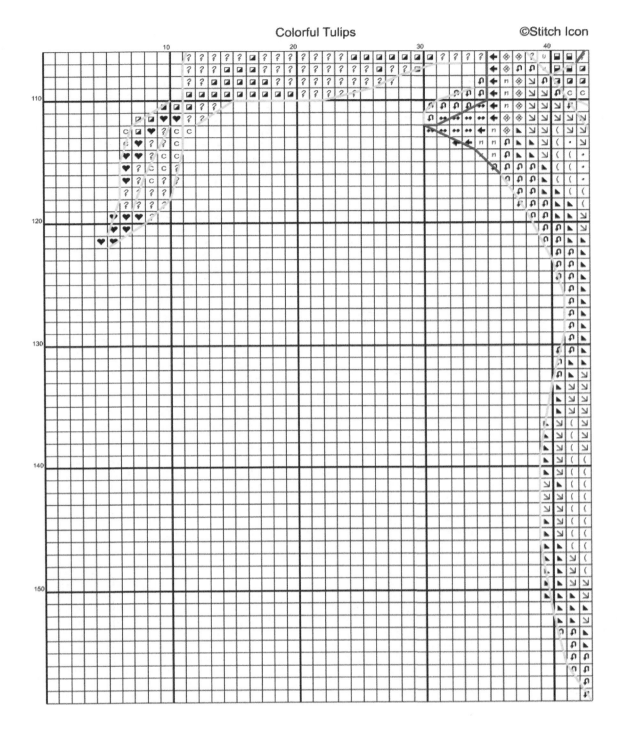

Colorful Tulips ©Stitch Icon

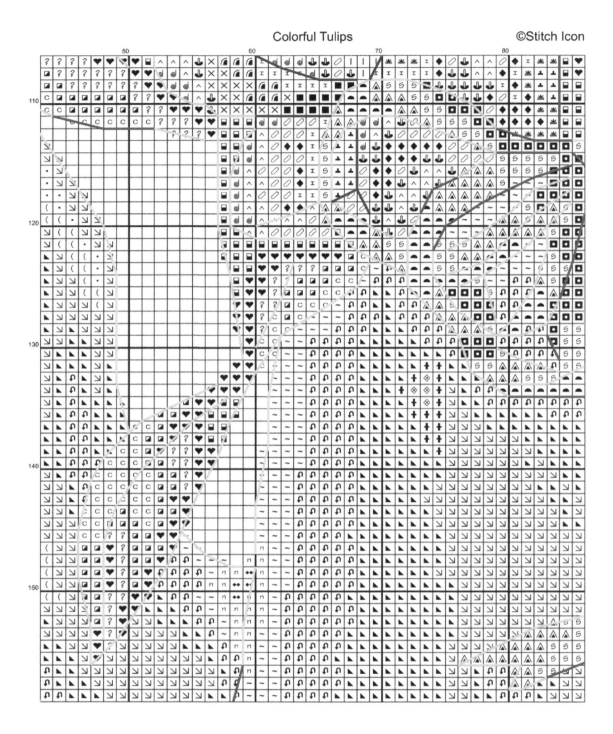

80

Colorful Tulips ©Stitch Icon

81

Colorful Tulips   ©Stitch Icon

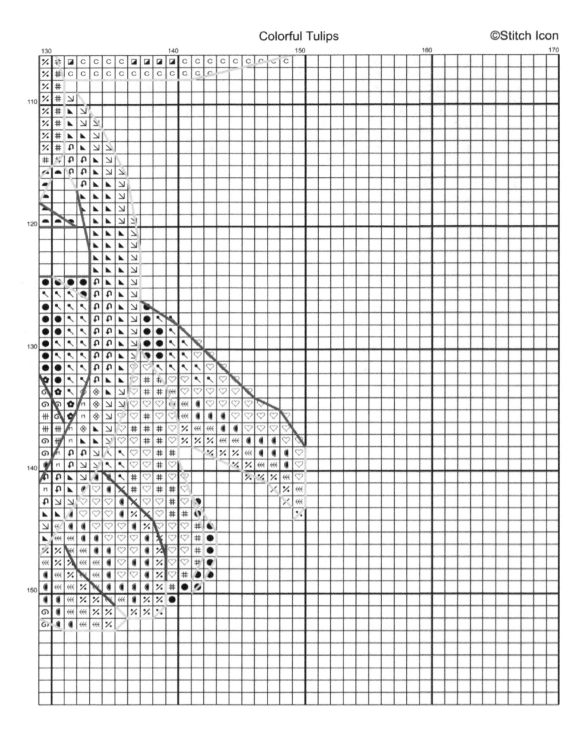

82

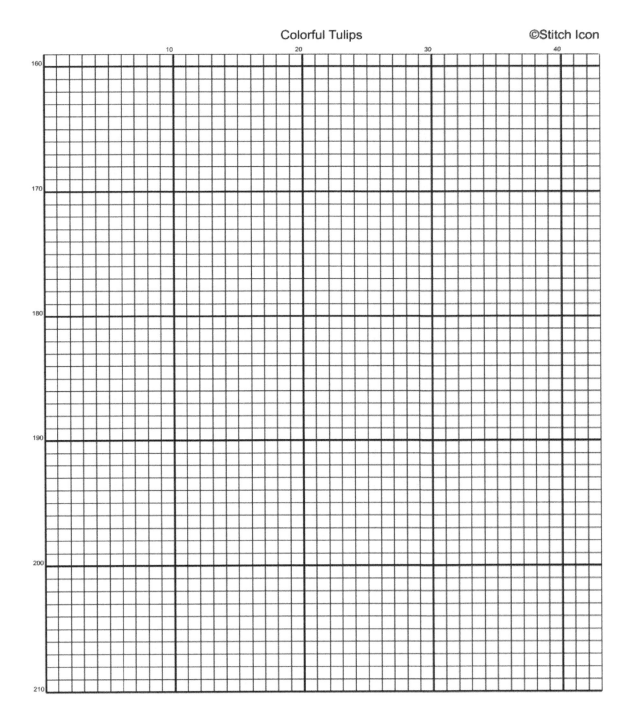

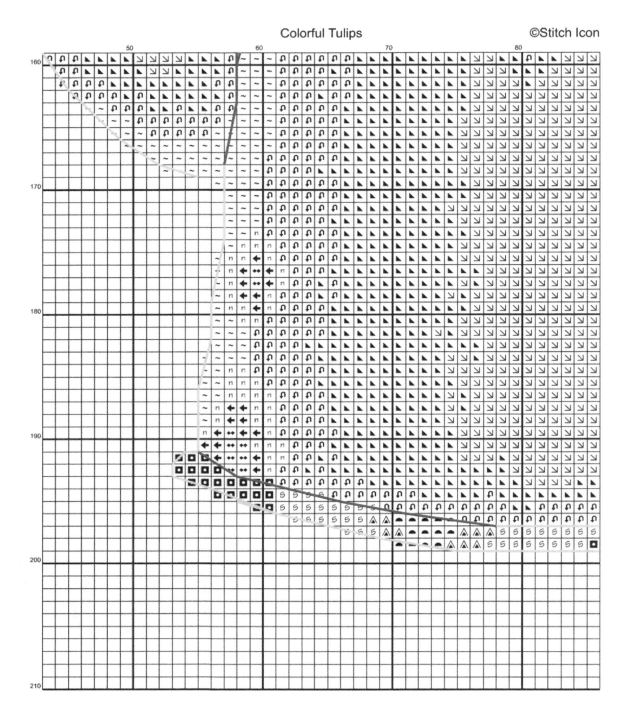

©Stitch Icon

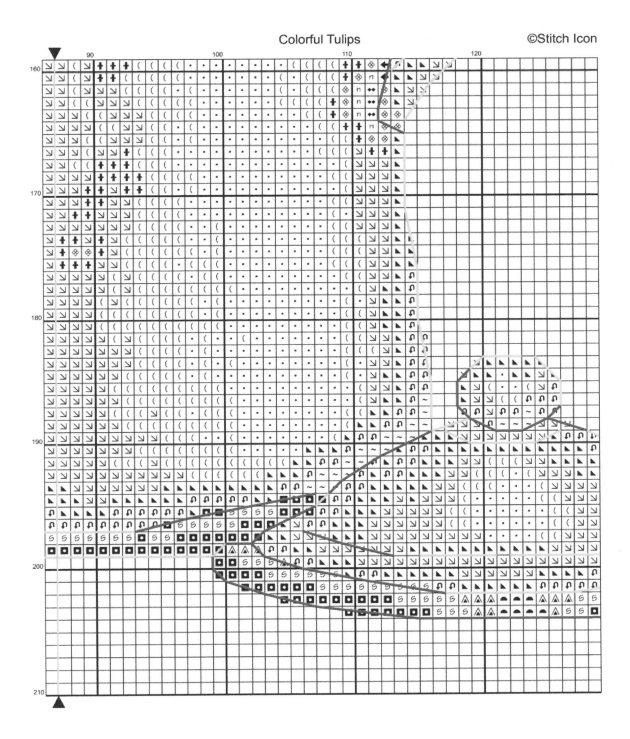

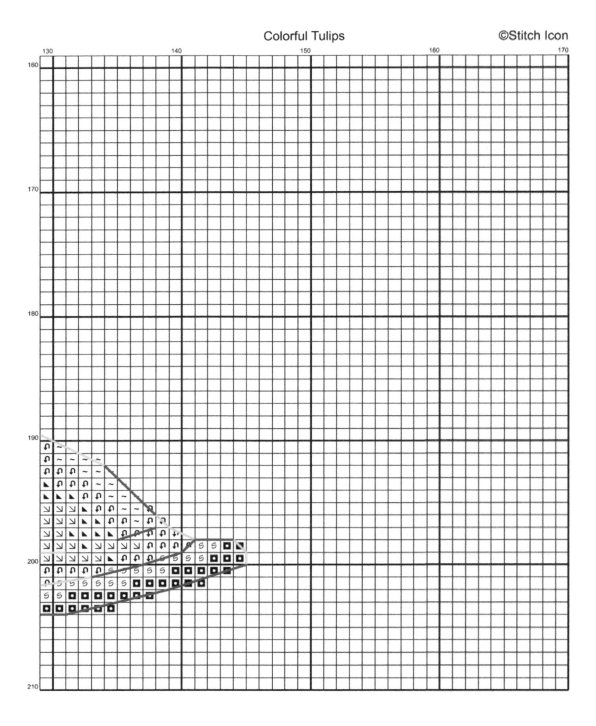

Colorful Tulips

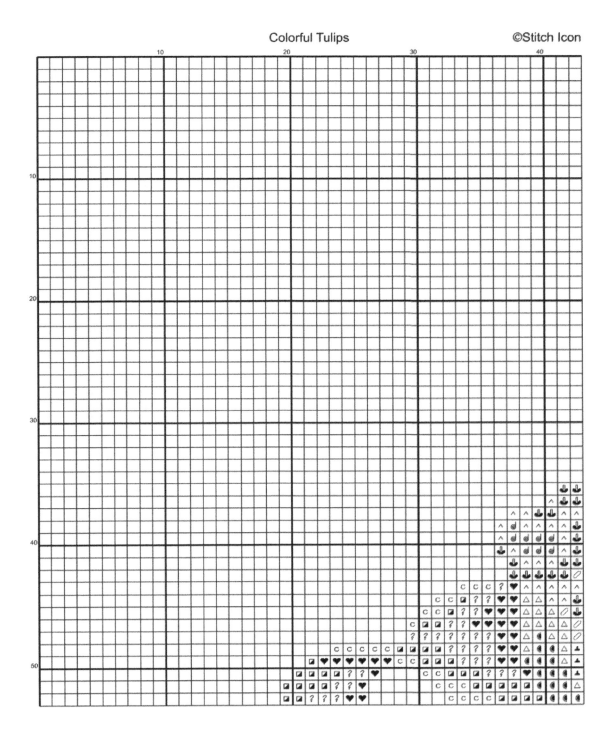

87

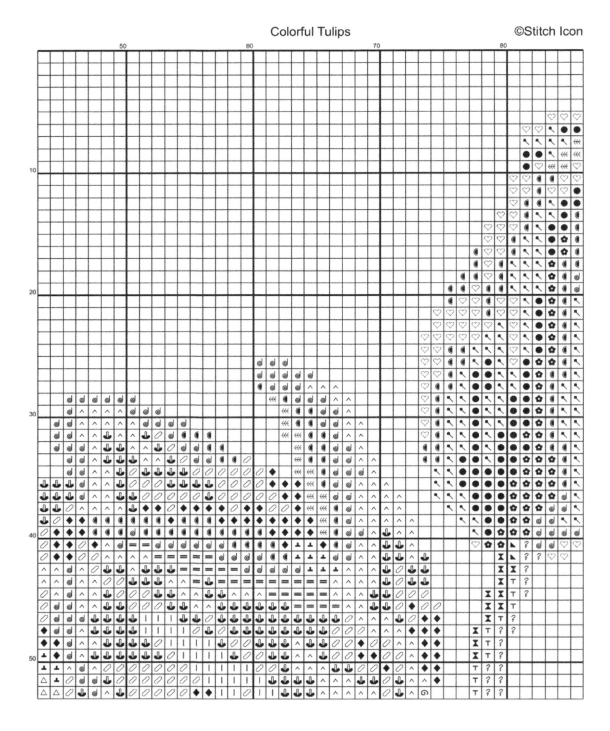

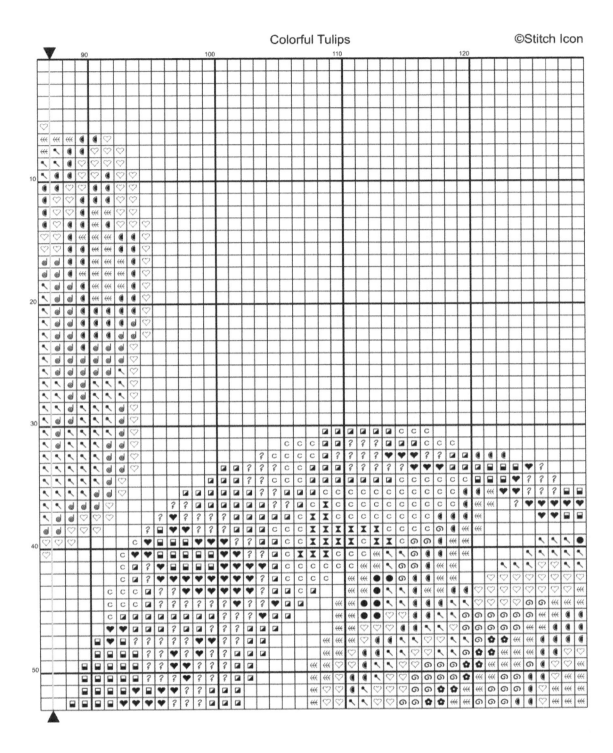

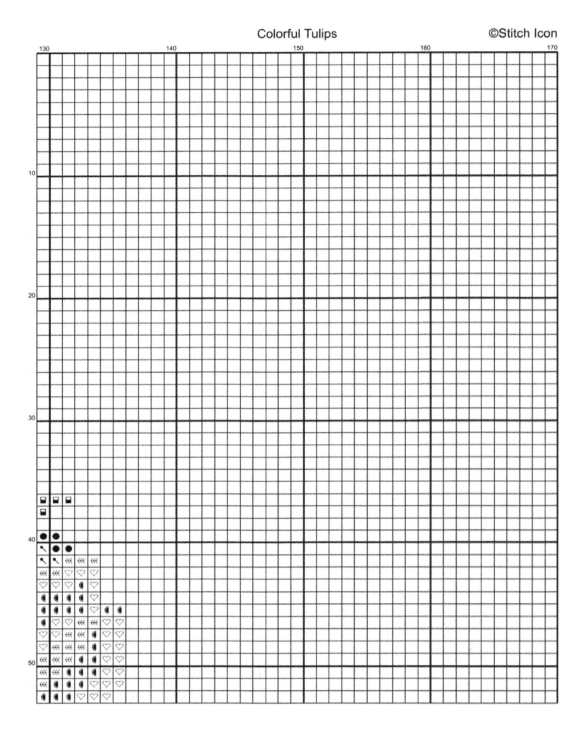

Colorful Tulips   ©Stitch Icon

90

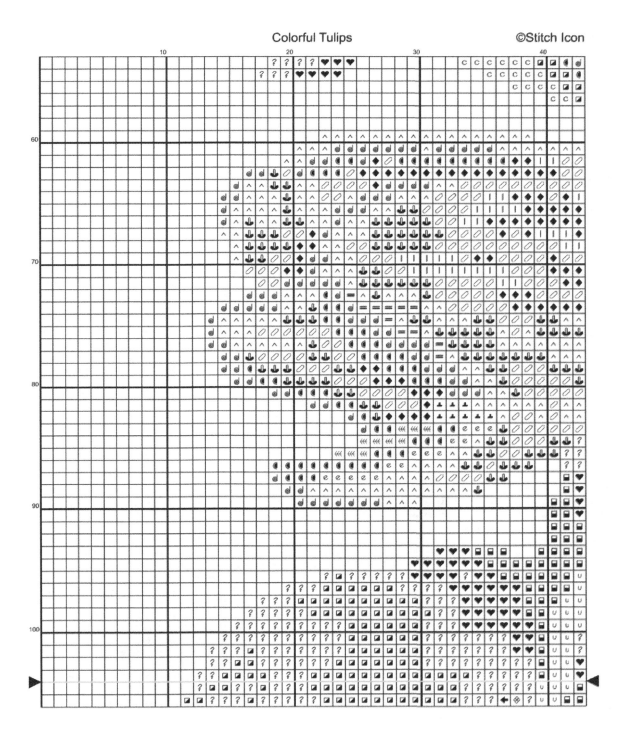

Colorful Tulips   ©Stitch Icon

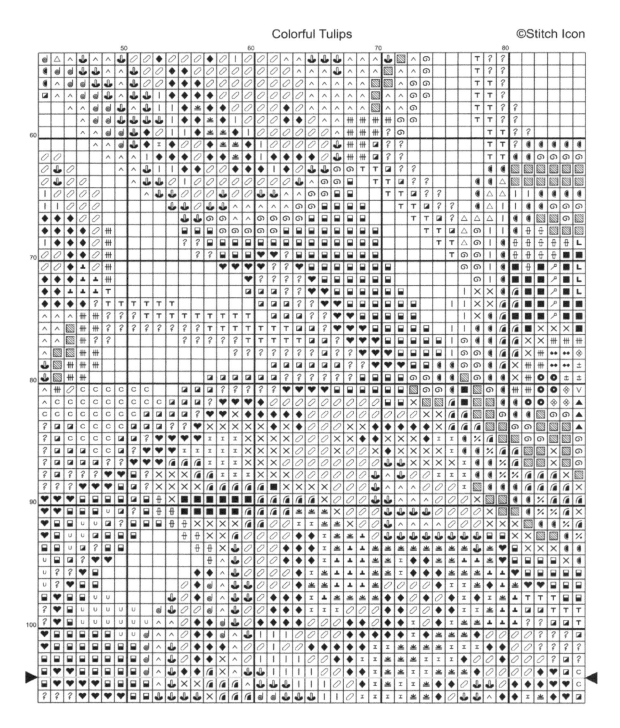

92

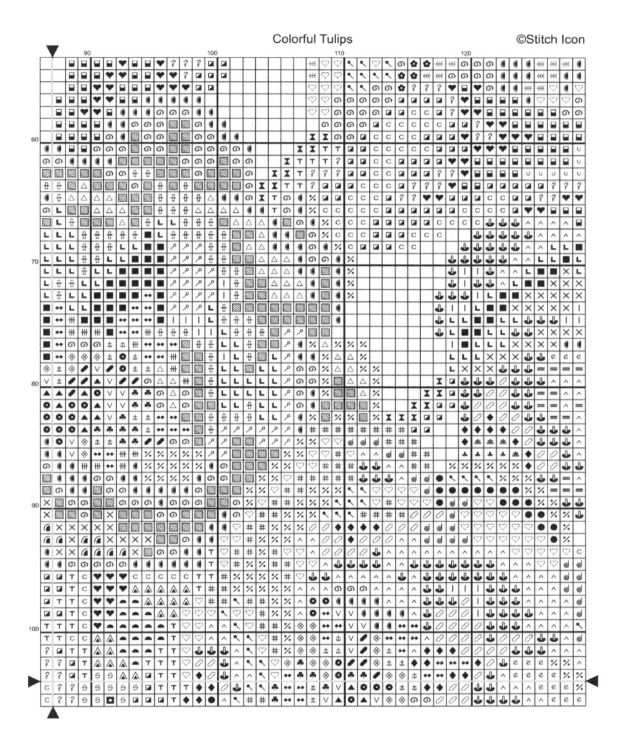

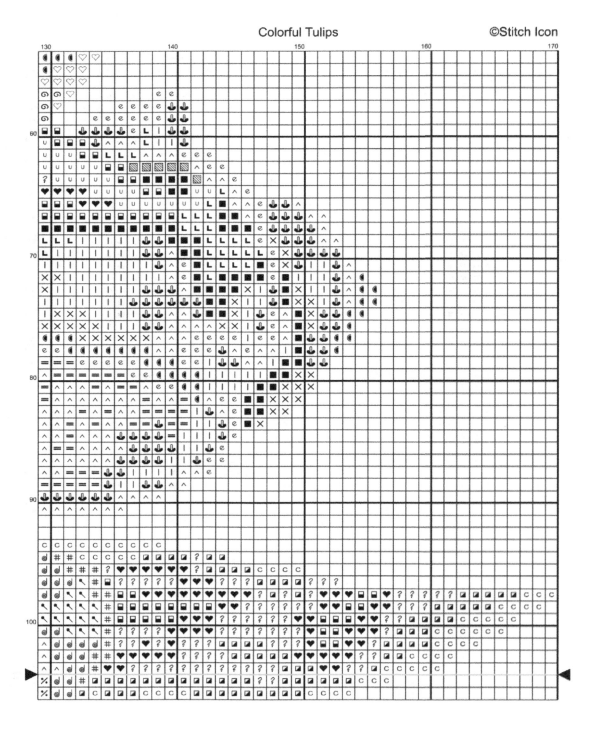

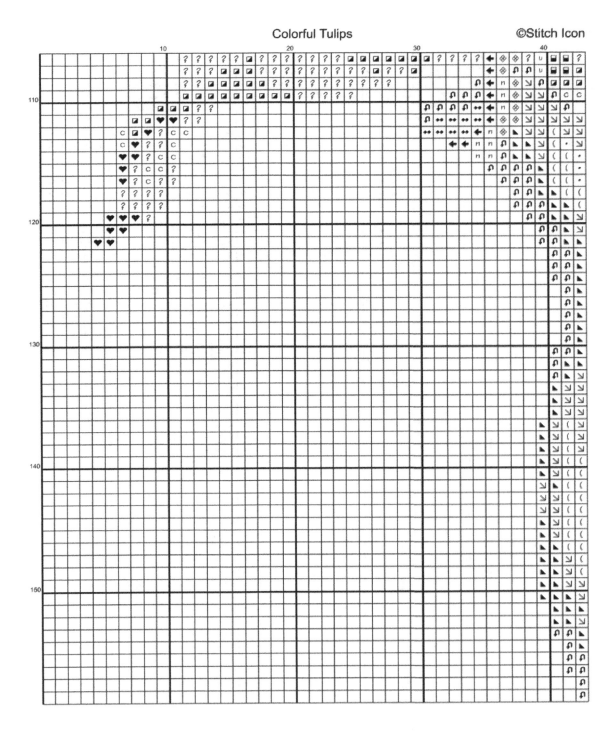

Colorful Tulips ©Stitch Icon

96

Colorful Tulips

©Stitch Icon

97

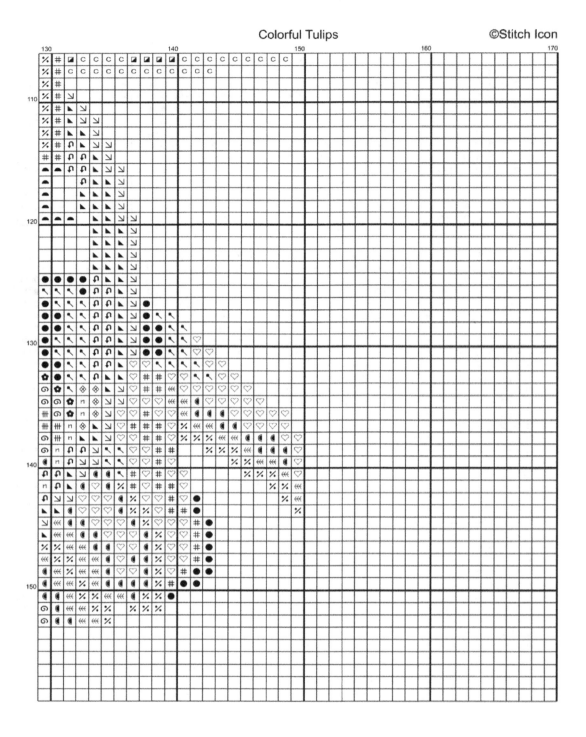

Colorful Tulips ©Stitch Icon

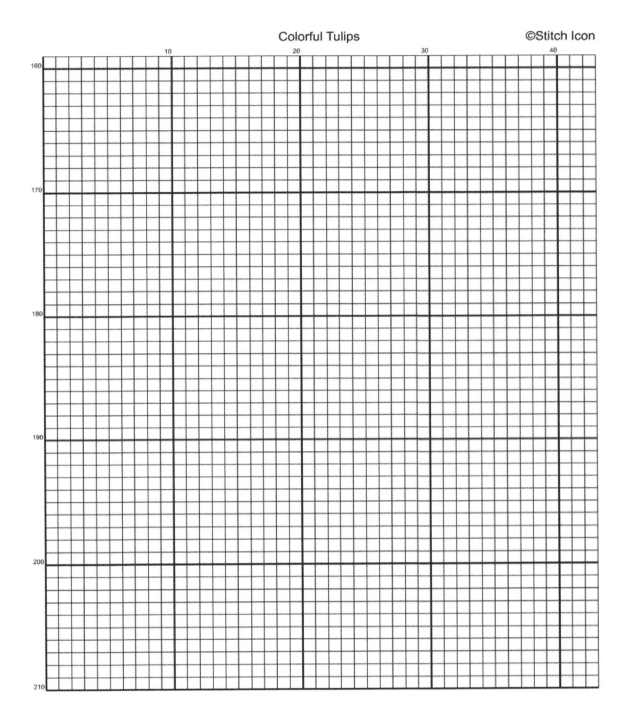

Colorful Tulips

©Stitch Icon

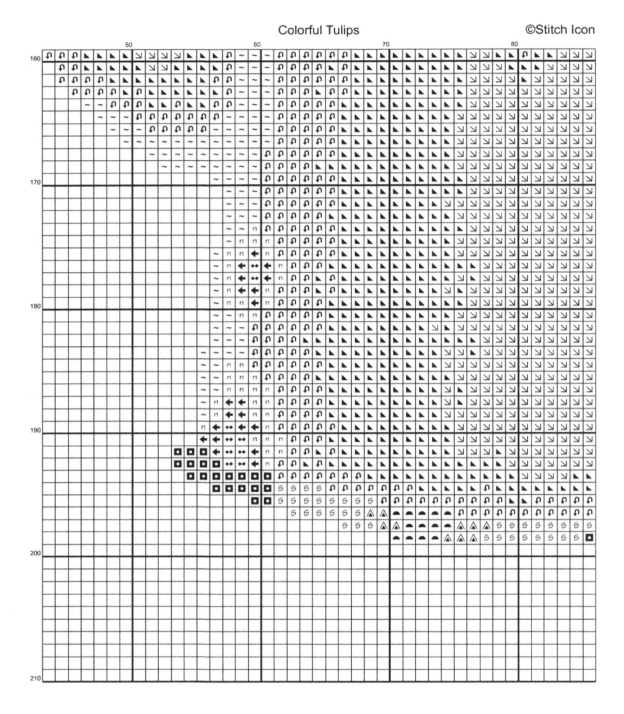

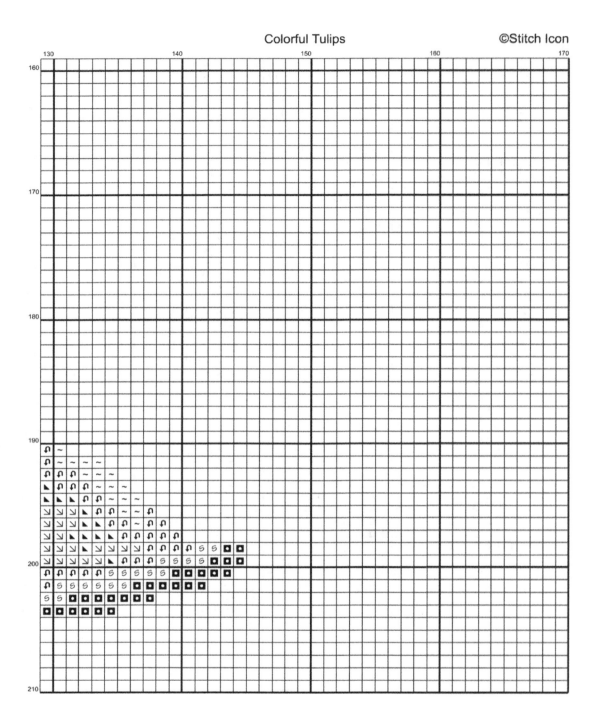

DAFFODILS IN POT

Overview

Palette: DMC
Colors: 48
Stitches used: full cross stitch, backstitch
Fabric: 14 Aida
Chart Size: 112 x 109 Stitches
Finished Size: 203 x 198 mm or 8.00 x 7.79 inch

Essence of Spring:
The Delicate Daffodils Cross-Stitch Marvel

Prepare to be captivated by the essence of spring as you embark on a stitching journey with the "Spring Flowers" pattern, featuring the enchanting "Daffodils in Pot" design. In this masterful creation, the artist has effortlessly captured the very essence of minimalism, showcasing the beauty of simplicity.

Measuring a mere 203 x 198 mm or 8.00 x 7.79 inches, this cross-stitch marvel may be the smallest project in our book, but its impact is anything but small. With remarkable skill, cross-stitch designer has brought to life the delicate charm of spring flowers blooming in a ceramic pot, using a palette of just 48 exquisite embroidery floss colors.

The fragile yellow daffodils and tender violets gracefully emerge from the fabric, as if transported from a watercolor painting onto your stitching canvas. Through carefully chosen hues, this composition radiates a natural vibrancy that effortlessly blends with any modern interior, subtly enhancing its beauty without overpowering it.

In this homage to simplicity, the designer has harnessed the power of colors, transforming threads into an enchanting tapestry of tranquility. Each stitch is a brushstroke, delicately bringing forth the spirit of spring, filling your space with the gentle allure of blooming flowers and the promise of new beginnings.

Thread Length Table (DMC # / Length, meters)

DMC 10 - 3,87	DMC 369 - 4,12	DMC 726 - 1,51	DMC 3354 - 0,42
DMC 15 - 5,7	DMC 470 - 0,75	DMC 760 - 0,11	DMC 3364 - 0,55
DMC 151 - 0,14	DMC 471 - 5,67	DMC 761 - 4,21	DMC 3688 - 1,09
DMC 152 - 2,13	DMC 472 - 3,93	DMC 954 - 1,08	DMC 3713 - 4,34
DMC 160 - 0,31	DMC 554 - 0,13	DMC 963 - 0,58	DMC 3727 - 0,22
DMC 208 - 0,14	DMC 562 - 2,6	DMC 966 - 0,36	DMC 3750 - 1,14
DMC 209 - 0,49	DMC 563 - 3,16	DMC 992 - 0,46	DMC 3823 - 8,93
DMC 223 - 4,27	DMC 564 - 0,21	DMC 995 - 0,28	DMC 3837 - 0,18
DMC 310 - 24,39	DMC 712 - 11	DMC 3047 - 14,24	DMC 3846 - 1,08
DMC 316 - 5,76	DMC 721 - 0,43	DMC 3078 - 1,49	DMC 3854 - 1,67
DMC 318 - 4,42	DMC 722 - 0,03	DMC 3326 - 3,1	DMC 3865 - 1,06
DMC 368 - 3,22	DMC 725 - 2,38	DMC 3348 - 0,56	DMC 3866 - 9,58

Instructions and Symbol Key for Design "Spring Flowers"

Fabric: **14** count White Aida

Stitches: 112 x 109   **Size:** 8.00 x 7.79 inches or 20.32 x 19.78 cm

Colours: DMC

Use **2** strands of thread for cross stitch

Sym	No.		Sym	No.
∞	10		=	15
//	151		⬚	152
/	160		#	208
↑	209		H	223
□	310		@	316
⚓	368		+	369
♥	470		e	471
Y	472		✿	554
△	562		$	563
✿	564		◖	712
✖	721		%	722
⊕	725		▨	726
○	760		←	761
Z	954		••	963
□	966		□	992
C	995		~	3047
8	3078		♡	3326
☽	3348		✹	3354
⊘	3364		◆	3688
⋂	3713		(	3727
✚	3750		◪	3823
◢	3837		◖	3846
⏝	3854		U	3865
6	3866			

Backstitch

Use **1** strand of thread for backstitch

———————— DMC 310
———————— DMC 318

Use 2 strands of thread for backstitch
———————— DMC 310

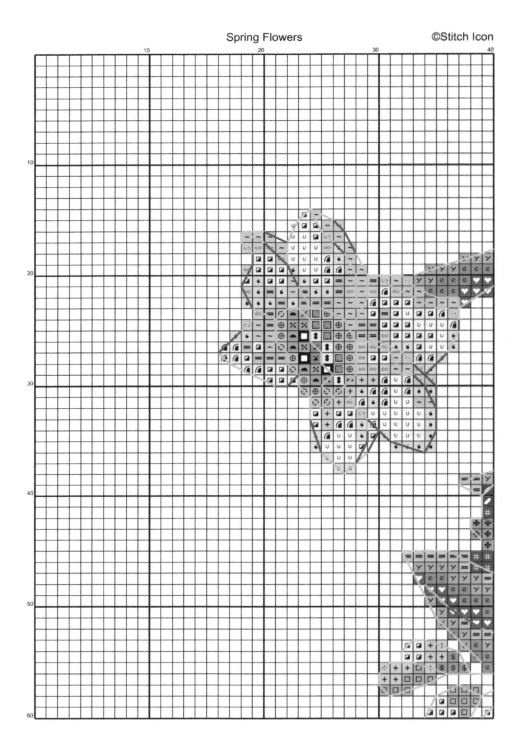

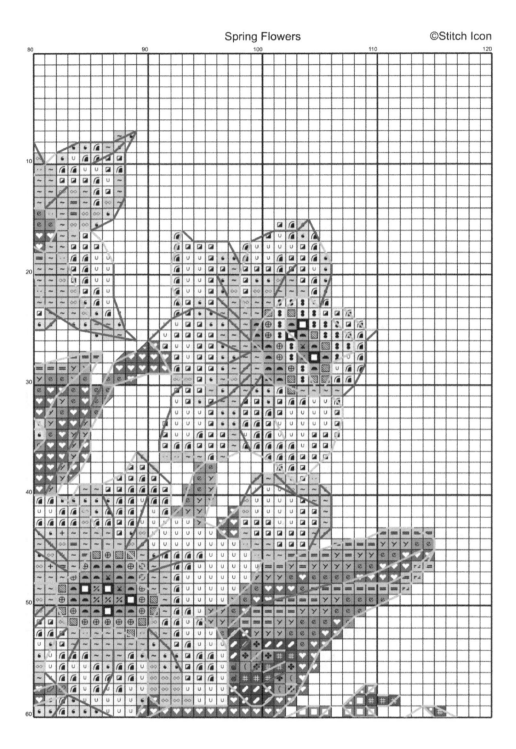

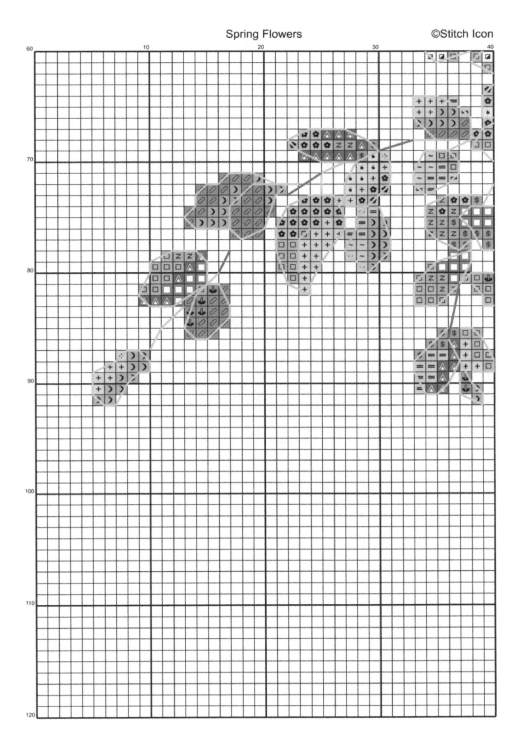

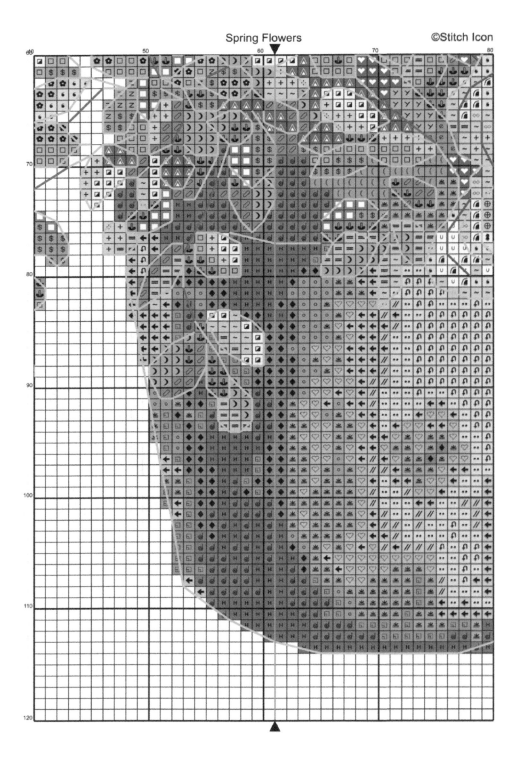

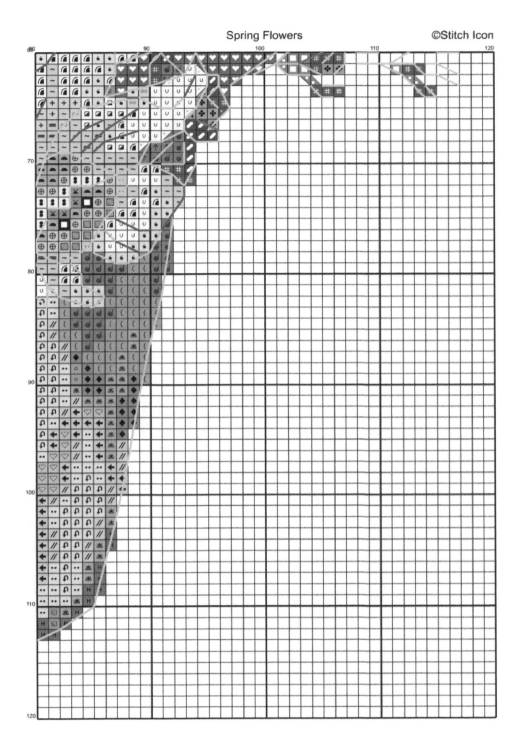

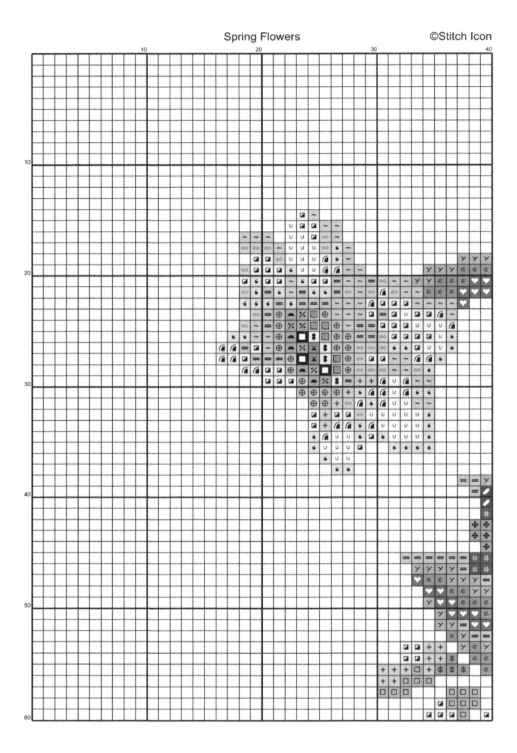

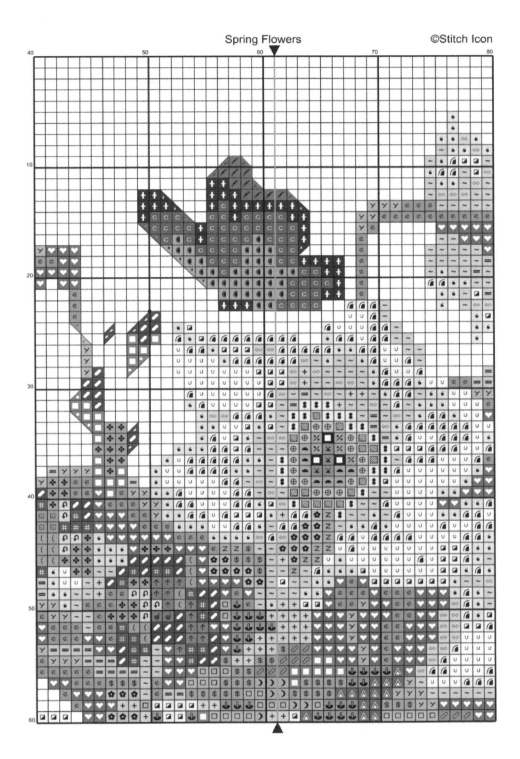

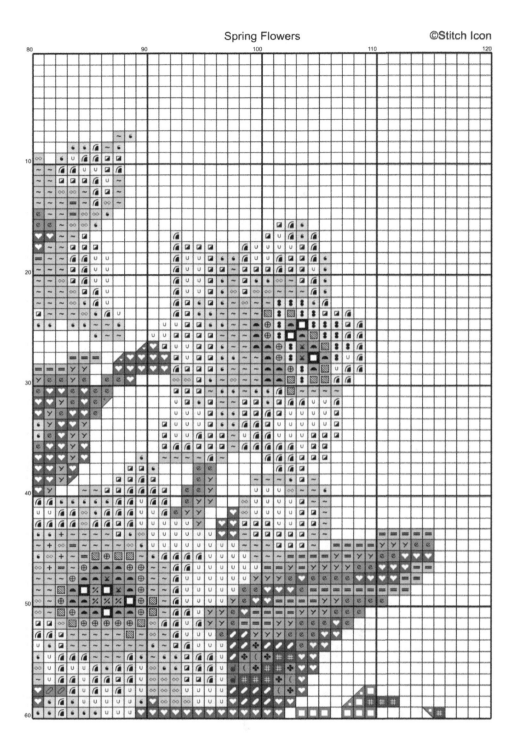

Spring Flowers

©Stitch Icon

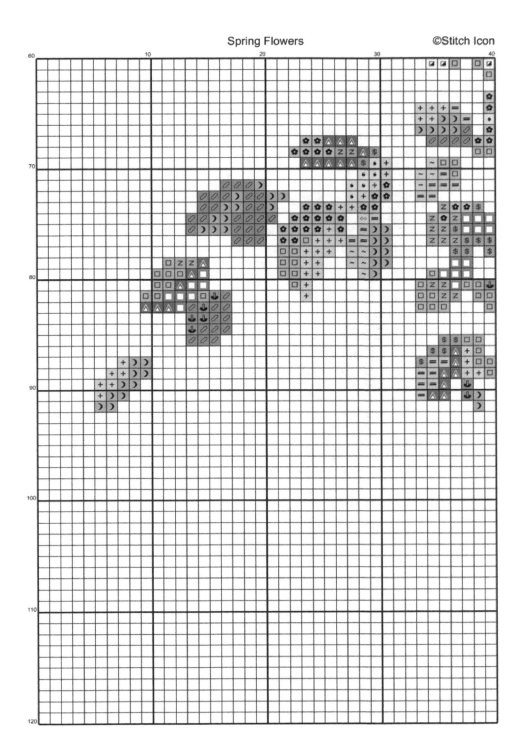

115

©Stitch Icon

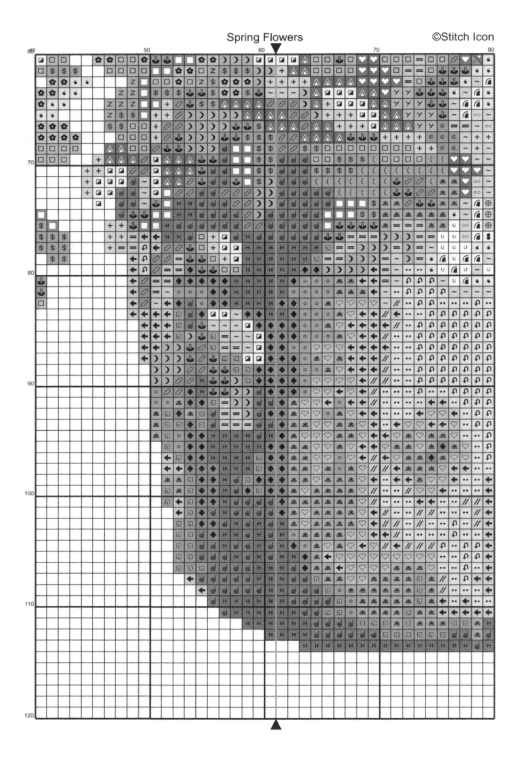

Spring Flowers   ©Stitch Icon

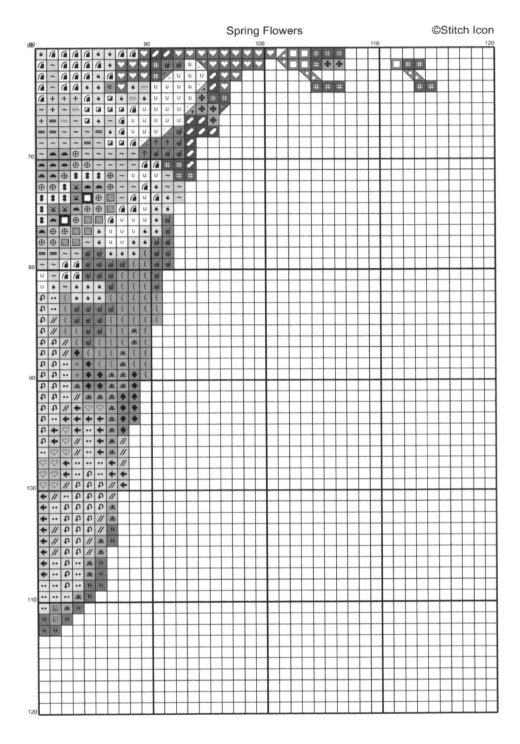

Instructions and Symbol Key for Design "Spring Flowers"

Fabric: 14 count White Aida

Stitches: 112 x 109   **Size:**   8.00 x 7.79 inches or 20.32 x 19.78 cm

Colours: DMC

Use **2** strands of thread for cross stitch

Sym	No.	Sym	No.
∞∞	10	=	15
//	151	⊡	152
⫽	160	#	208
↑	209	H	223
■	310	⊌	316
⬇	368	+	369
♥	470	e	471
Y	472	♣	554
⚠	562	$	563
✿	564	◪	712
✗	721	⁒	722
⊕	725	▨	726
○	760	←	761
Z	954	‥	963
□	966	■	992
c	995	~	3047
⁑	3078	♡	3326
⟩	3348	⚓	3354
⬭	3364	◆	3688
∩	3713	(	3727
✝	3750	◪	3823
✎	3837	◖	3846
◠	3854	U	3865
˙	3866		

Backstitch

Use **1** strand of thread for backstitch

——————— DMC 310
——————— DMC 318

Use 2 strands of thread for backstitch

——————— DMC 310

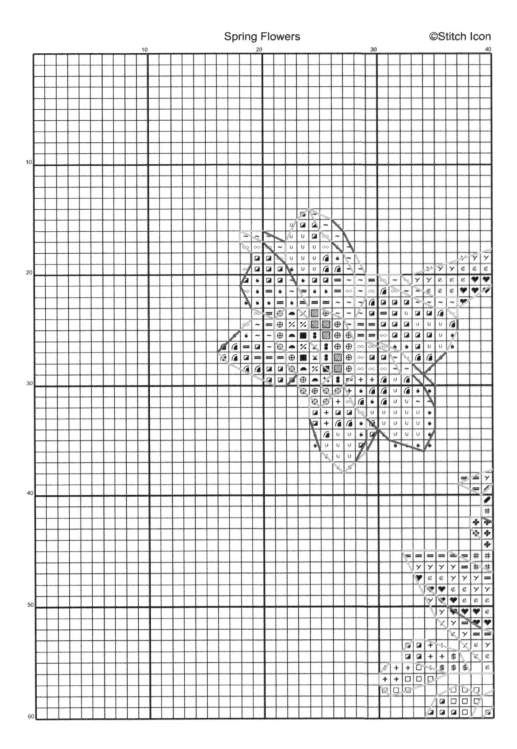

Spring Flowers   ©Stitch Icon

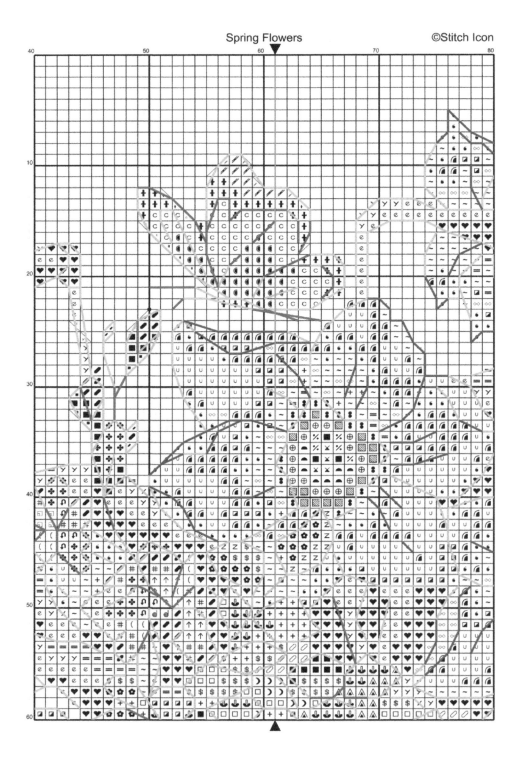

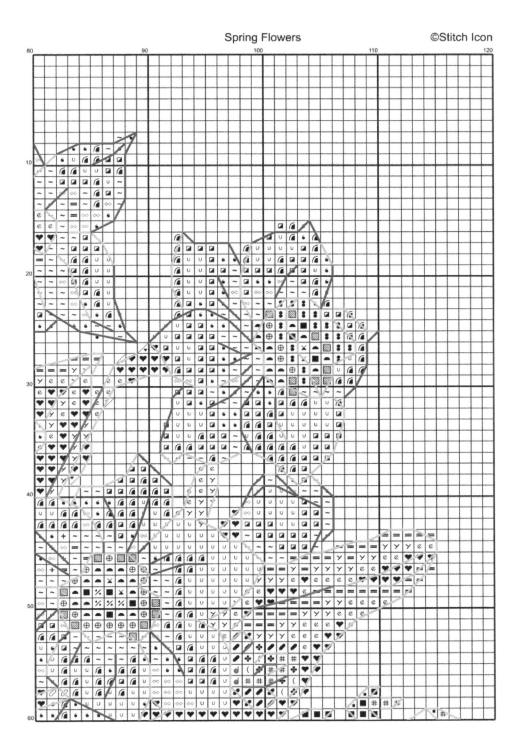

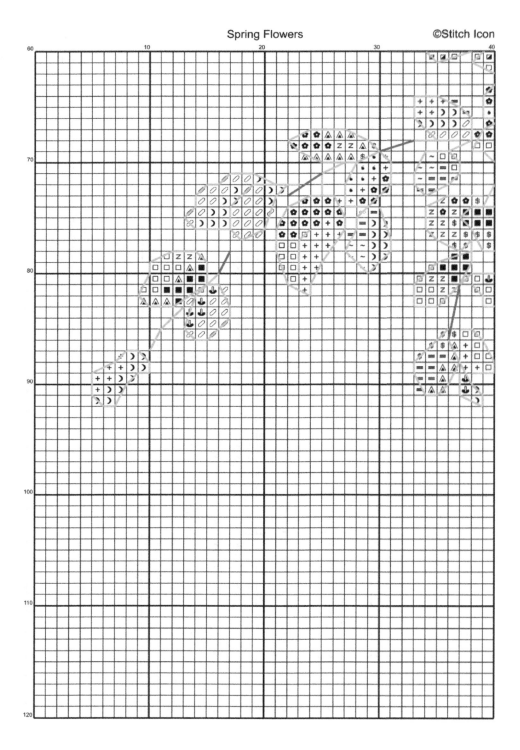

Spring Flowers   ©Stitch Icon

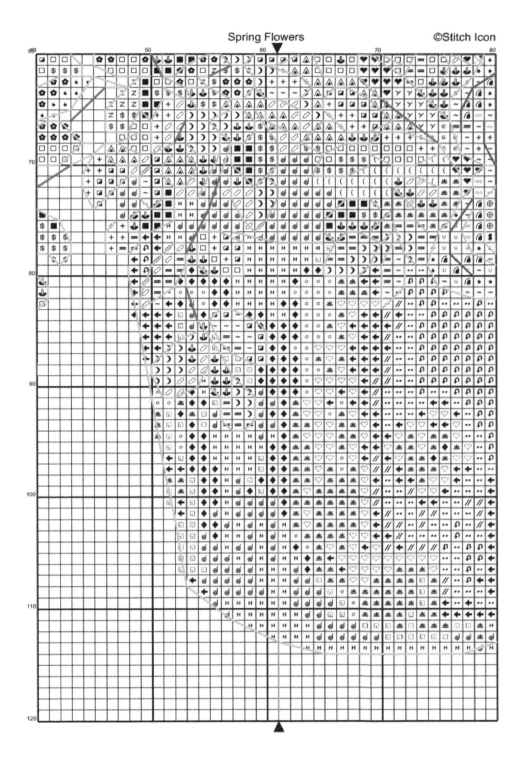

123

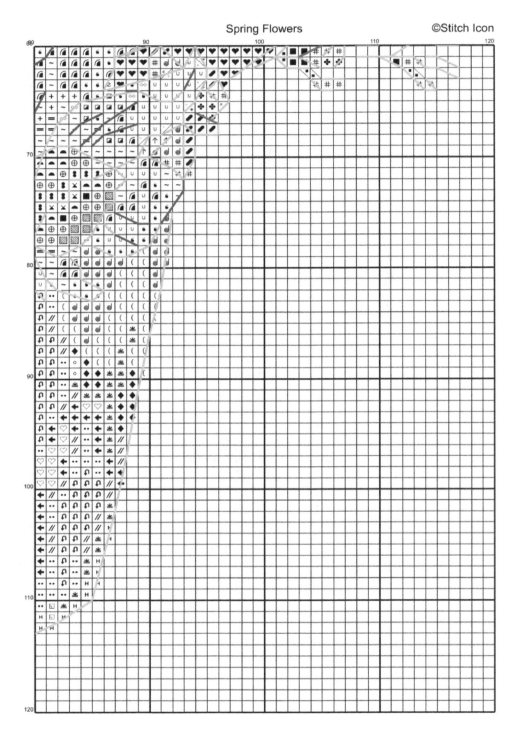

124

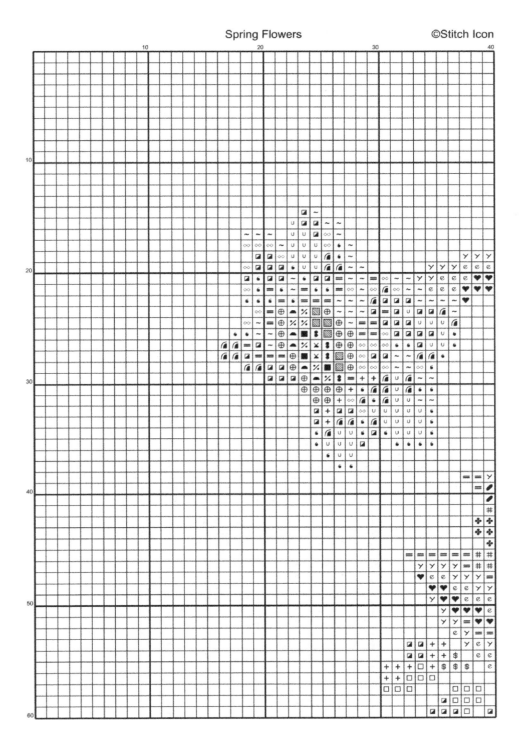

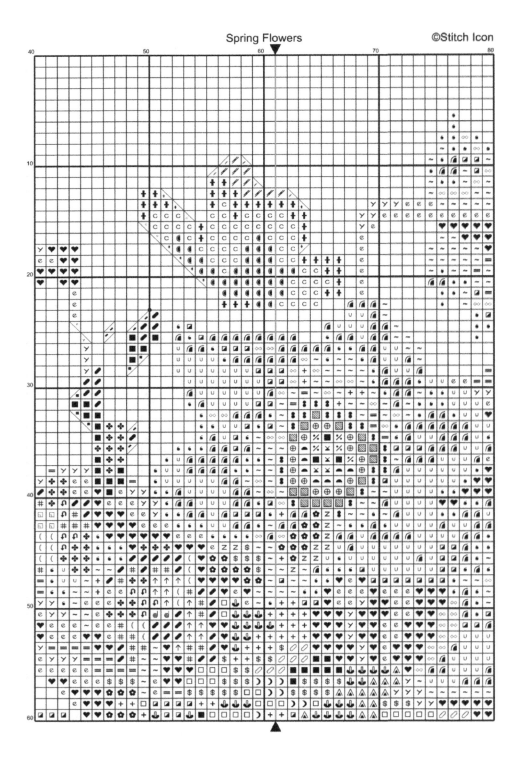

126

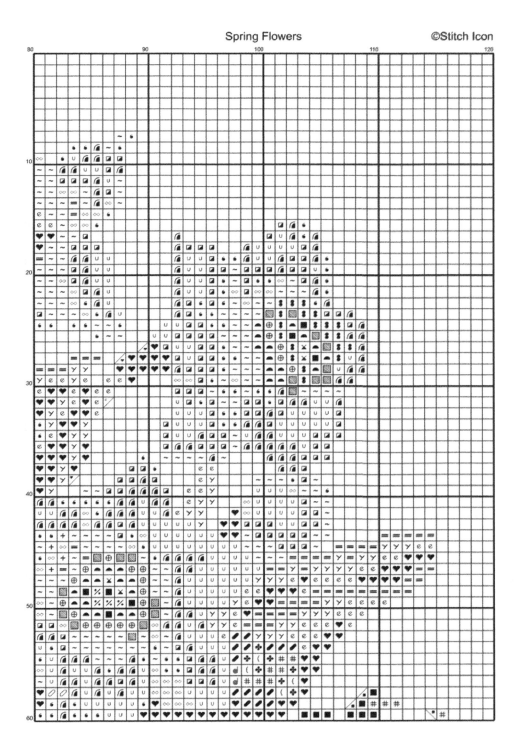

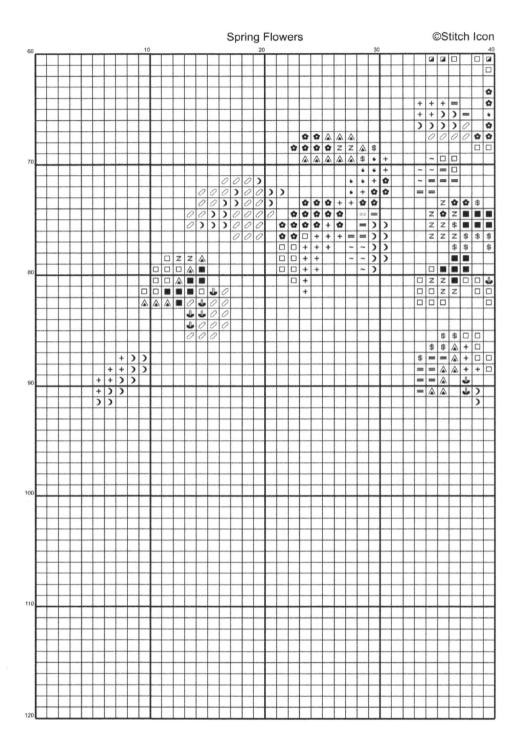

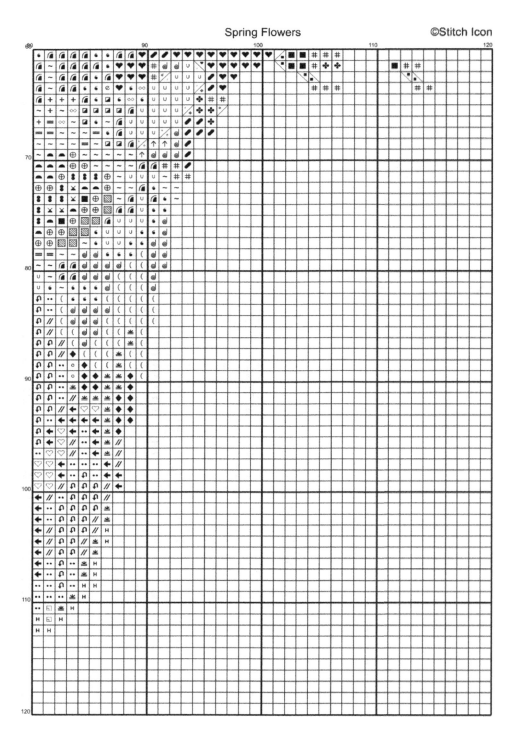

130

COLORFUL AUTUMN BOUQUET

<u>Overview</u>

Palette: DMC
Colors: 53
Stitches used: full cross stitch, backstitch
Fabric: 14 Aida
Chart Size: 248 x 123 Stitches
Finished Size: 450 x 223 mm or 17.71 x 8.79 inch

Autumn's Tapestry: A Cross-Stitch Ode to Nature's Beauty

Immerse yourself in the enchanting allure of autumn with the "Colorful Autumn Bouquet" cross-stitch pattern. This exquisite design captures the essence of the season, showcasing a harmonious blend of vibrant yellows, rich reds, soothing grays, and lush greens.

With its generous stitch size of 450 x 223 mm or 17.71 x 8.79 inches, this pattern offers a canvas that allows you to explore the intricate details of autumn's opulent display. As you embark on this stitching journey, you'll be transported to a world where vibrant foliage dances across unseen surfaces, inviting you to revel in the splendor of the season.

Delight in the interplay of colors as you bring the "Colorful Autumn Bouquet" to life. Shades of yellow exude warmth and joy, while hints of red and gray hint at nature's graceful transitions. The backdrop of lush greens sets the stage, mirroring the foliage that serves as the foundation for this captivating composition.

Experience the magic of autumn with each stitch, as threads intertwine to form a captivating tapestry that celebrates the abundance and beauty of this cherished time of year. Each stitch is a brushstroke that weaves a story of nature's artistry, allowing you to revel in the captivating beauty of autumn's embrace.

Thread Length Table (DMC # / Length, meters)

DMC 3 - 4,99	DMC 349 - 5,3	DMC 761 - 0,36	DMC 3072 - 15,47
DMC 4 - 5,45	DMC 414 - 0,37	DMC 762 - 1,15	DMC 3354 - 2,51
DMC 18 - 1,39	DMC 415 - 4,4	DMC 780 - 7,87	DMC 3363 - 0,74
DMC 23 - 7,16	DMC 433 - 1,95	DMC 782 - 1,48	DMC 3371 - 43,74
DMC 24 - 2,72	DMC 444 - 4,55	DMC 815 - 2,2	DMC 3688 - 0,19
DMC 27 - 0,42	DMC 452 - 0,57	DMC 869 - 6,38	DMC 3722 - 10,51
DMC 151 - 5,36	DMC 453 - 1,67	DMC 898 - 0,32	DMC 3726 - 5,64
DMC 152 - 2,94	DMC 522 - 2,63	DMC 919 - 1,82	DMC 3727 - 1,32
DMC 154 - 0,28	DMC 523 - 14,74	DMC 922 - 10,1	DMC 3802 - 0,54
DMC 168 - 13,14	DMC 524 - 9,87	DMC 927 - 0,26	DMC 3820 - 4,1
DMC 223 - 17,52	DMC 720 - 17,89	DMC 938 - 4,99	DMC 3824 - 0,5
DMC 307 - 2,57	DMC 722 - 1,82	DMC 3022 - 3,28	DMC 3852 - 32,85
DMC 315 - 9,52	DMC 728 - 2,34	DMC 3024 - 1,2	DMC 3865 - 8,7
			DMC 3866 - 5,39

Instructions and Symbol Key for Design "Colorful Autumn Bouquet"

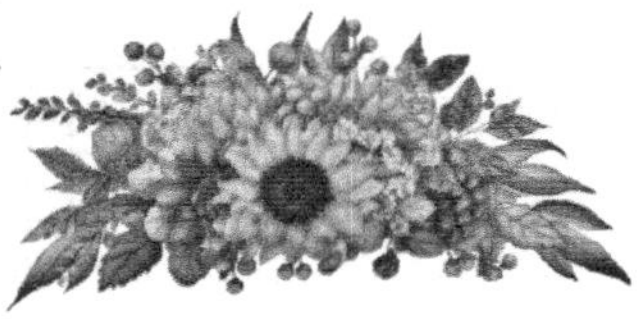

Fabric:	**14** count White Aida
Stitches:	248 x 123	**Size:** 17.71 x 8.79 inches or 44.99 x 22.32 cm
Colours:	DMC

Use **2** strands of thread for cross stitch

Sym	No.		Sym	No.
🅐	3		✹	4
e	18		Z	23
/	24		▼	27
⋘	151		U	152
▯	154		I	168
⚓	223		▨	307
^	315		C	349
V	414		?	415
L	433		◗	444
◀	452		♥	453
✕	522		↻	523
◕	524		◖	720
△	722		✖	728
⊕	761		~	762
◭	780		◣	782
▢	815		♡	869
‡	898		⅄	919
m	922		✿	927
◆	938		⬏	3022
◗	3024		⊙	3072
↴	3354		◢	3363
▮	3371		(	3688
⊞	3722		@	3726
⊘	3727		➡	3802
#	3820		◎	3824
◆◆	3852		·	3865
6	3866			

Backstitch

Use **1** strand of thread for backstitch

———————— DMC 869

———————— DMC 3371

Use 2 strands of thread for backstitch

———————— DMC 3371

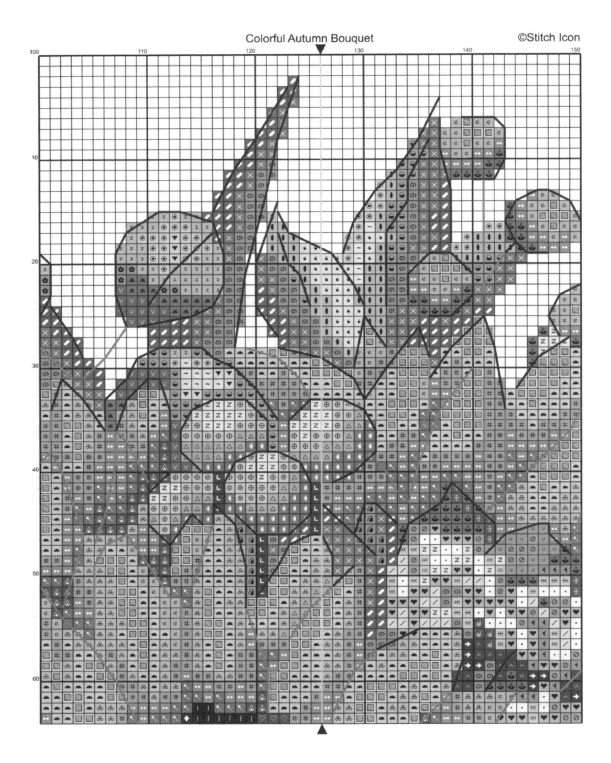

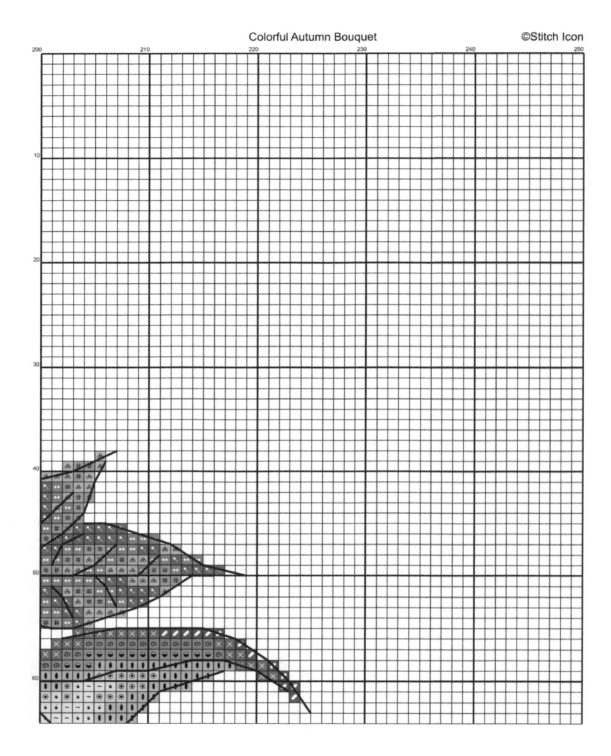

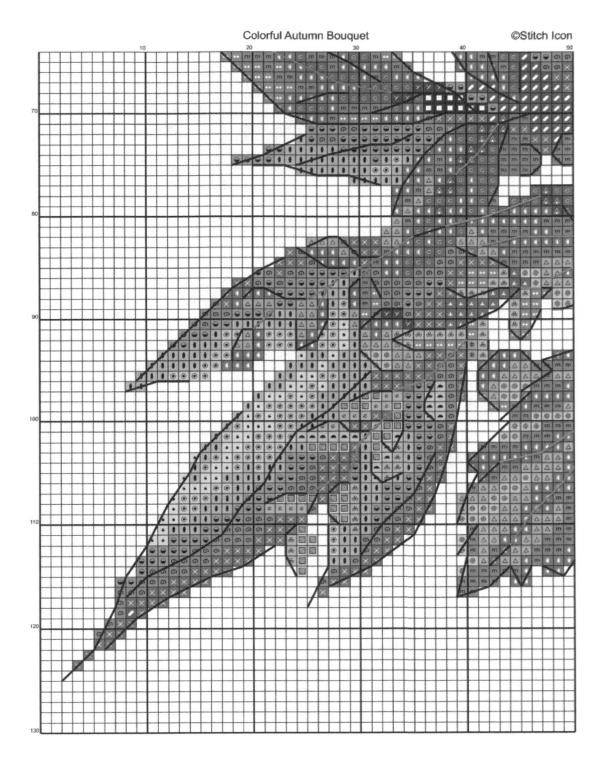

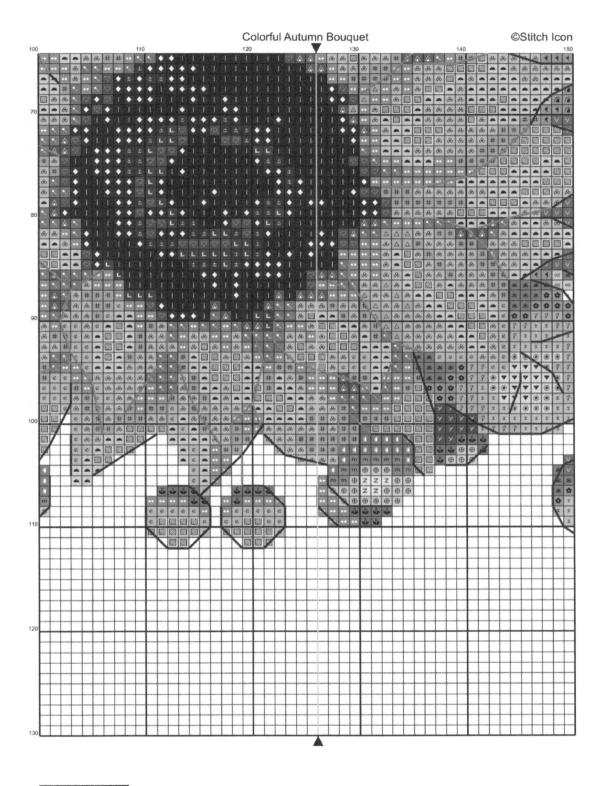

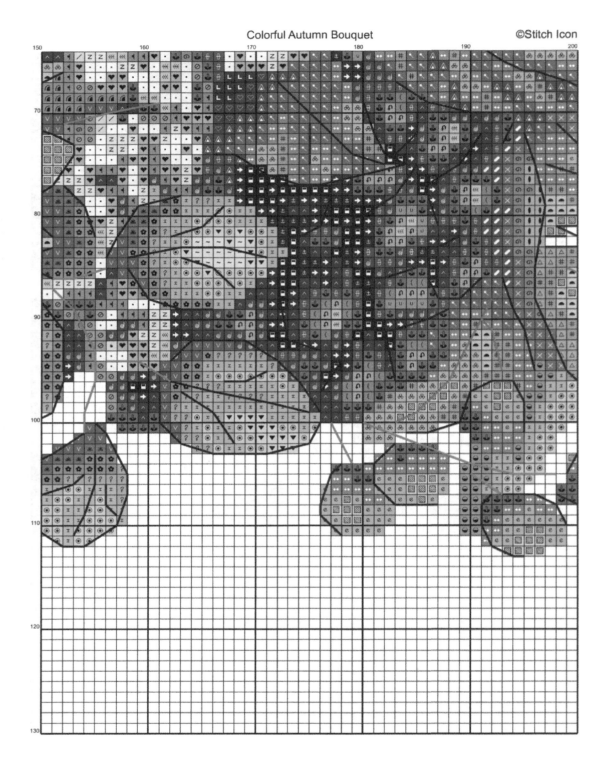

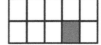

142

Colorful Autumn Bouquet

©Stitch Icon

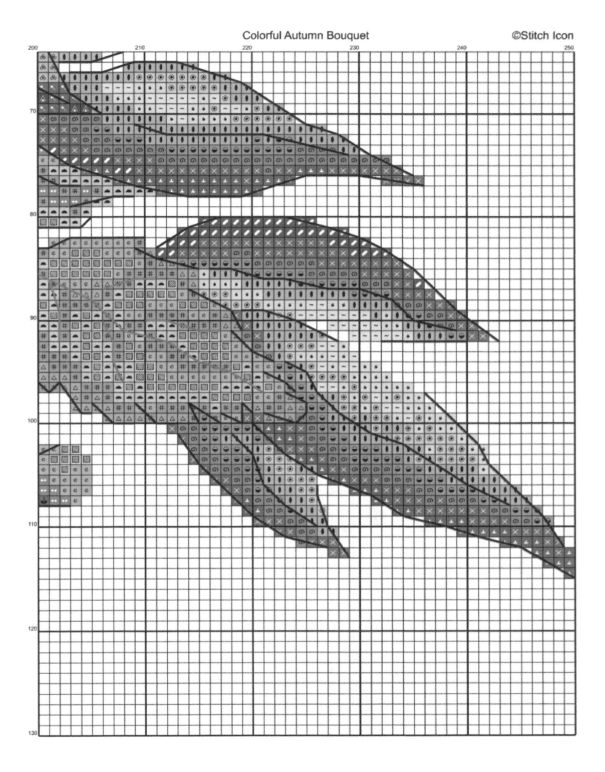

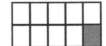

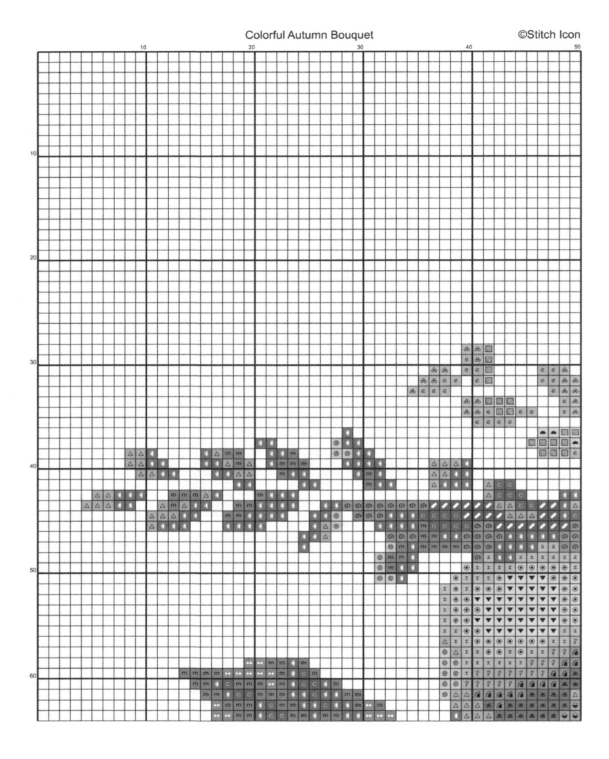

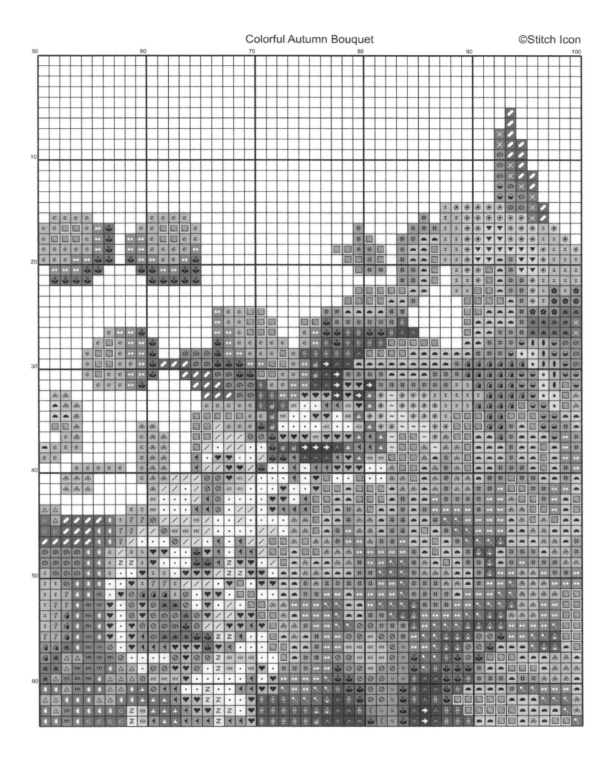

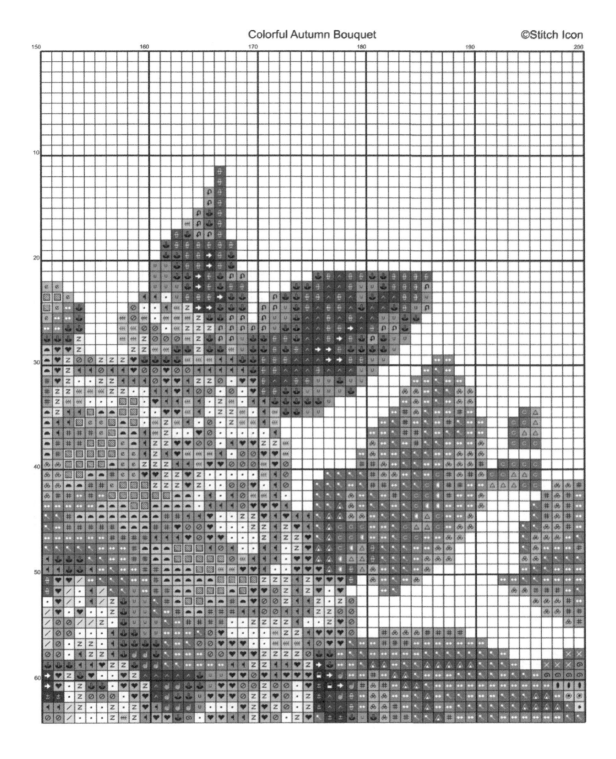

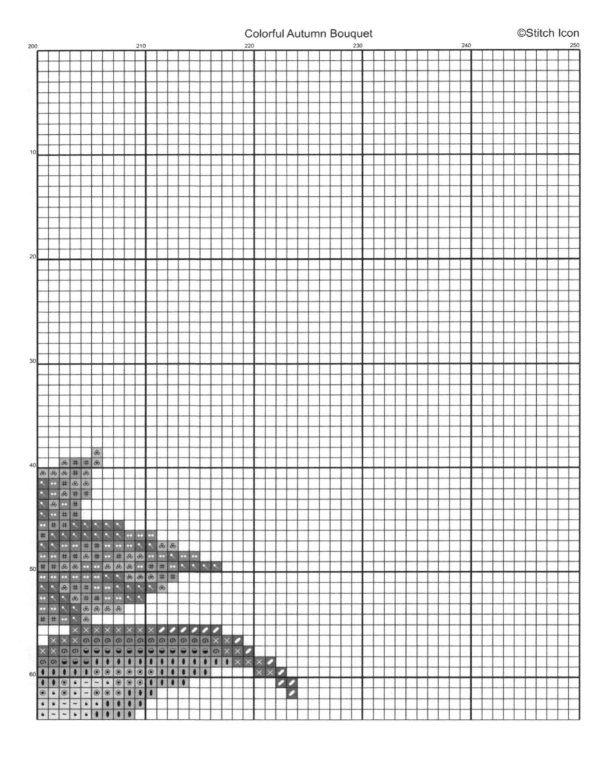

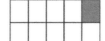

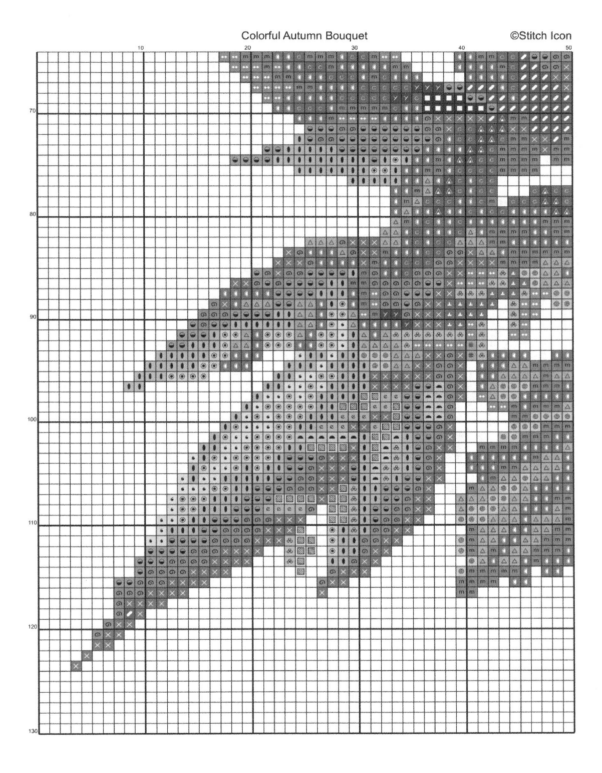

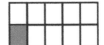

149

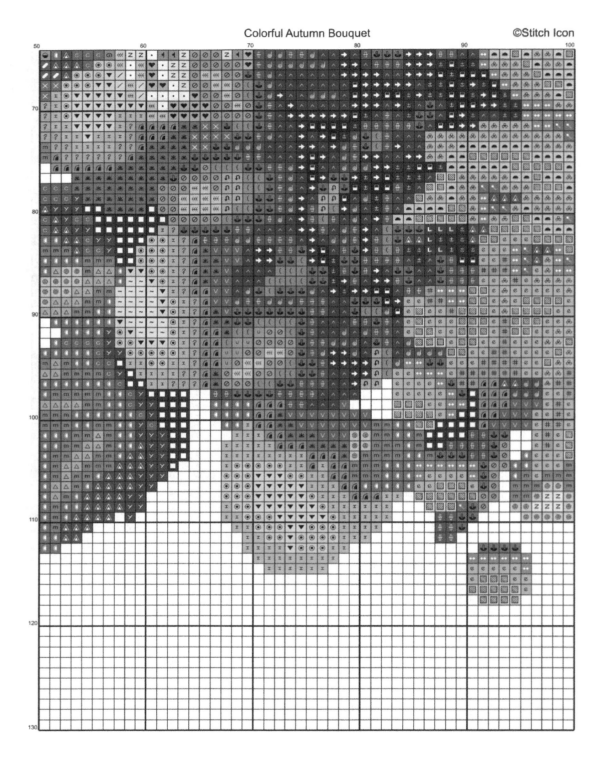

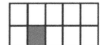

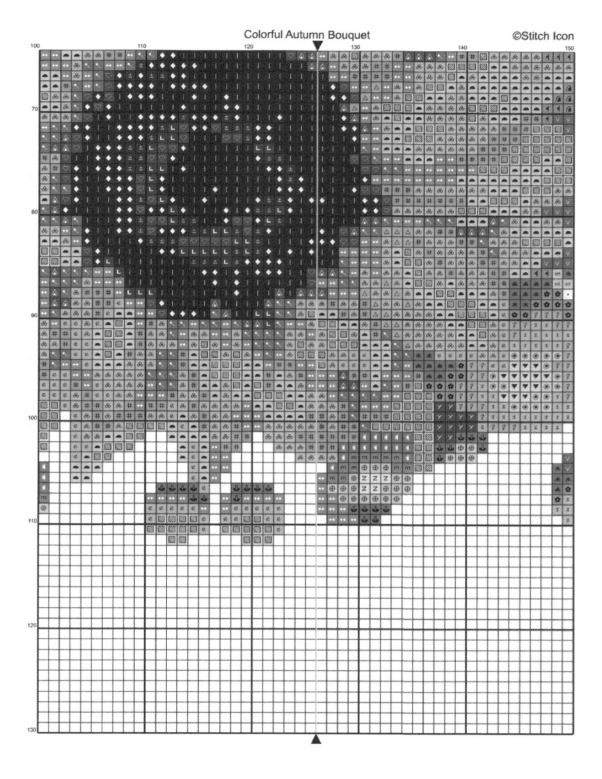

151

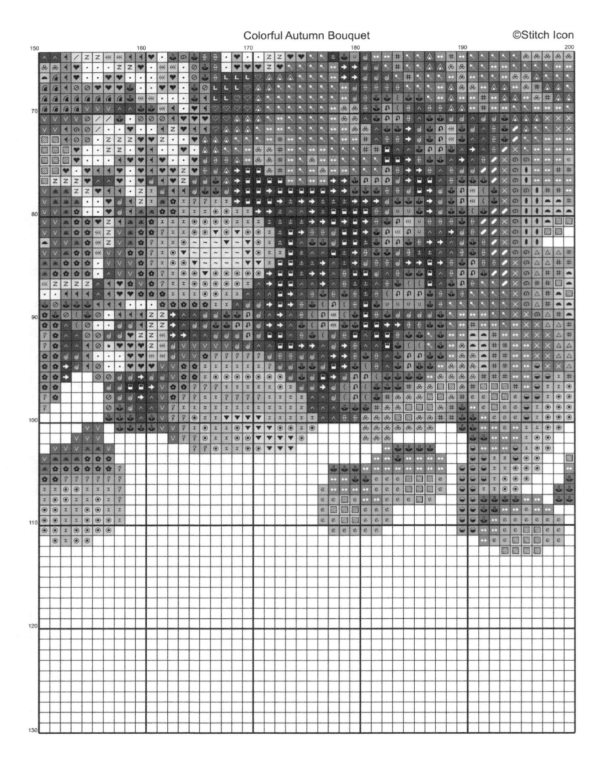

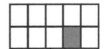

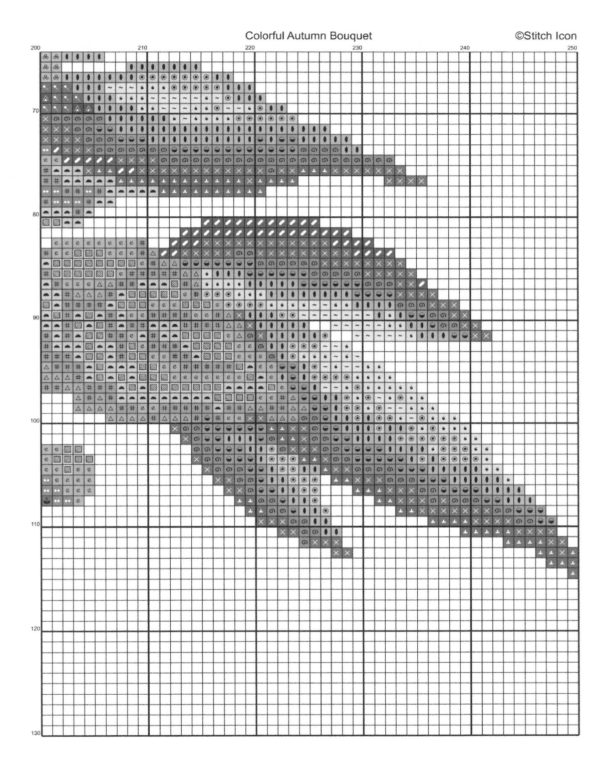

Instructions and Symbol Key for Design "Colorful Autumn Bouquet"

Fabric: 14 count White Aida

Stitches: 248 x 123   **Size:** 17.71 x 8.79 inches or 44.99 x 22.32 cm

Colours: DMC

Use **2** strands of thread for cross stitch

Sym	No.		Sym	No.
◖	3		✷	4
e	18		Z	23
∕	24		▼	27
⋘	151		U	152
▭	154		I	168
⚓	223		▨	307
∧	315		C	349
∨	414		?	415
L	433		◖	444
◀	452		♥	453
×	522		ග	523
◗	524		◖	720
△	722		⅋	728
⊕	761		~	762
◭	780		⬉	782
■	815		♡	869
∓	898		Y	919
m	922		✿	927
◆	938		⊥	3022
◗	3024		◉	3072
∩	3354		◗	3363
		3371		(	3688
⊹	3722		ⅆ	3726
⊘	3727		➜	3802
#	3820		◎	3824
↔	3852		·	3865
❛	3866			

Backstitch

Use **1** strand of thread for backstitch

——————— DMC 869

——————— DMC 3371

Use 2 strands of thread for backstitch

——————— DMC 3371

155

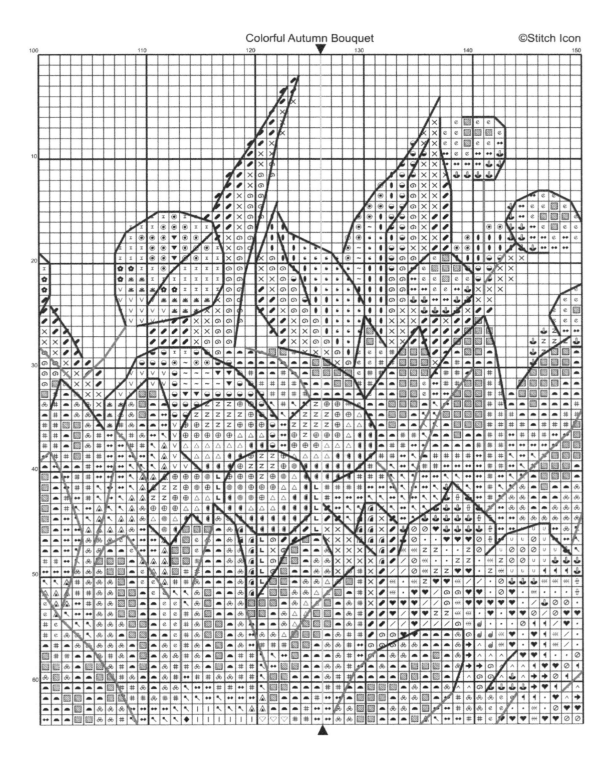

157

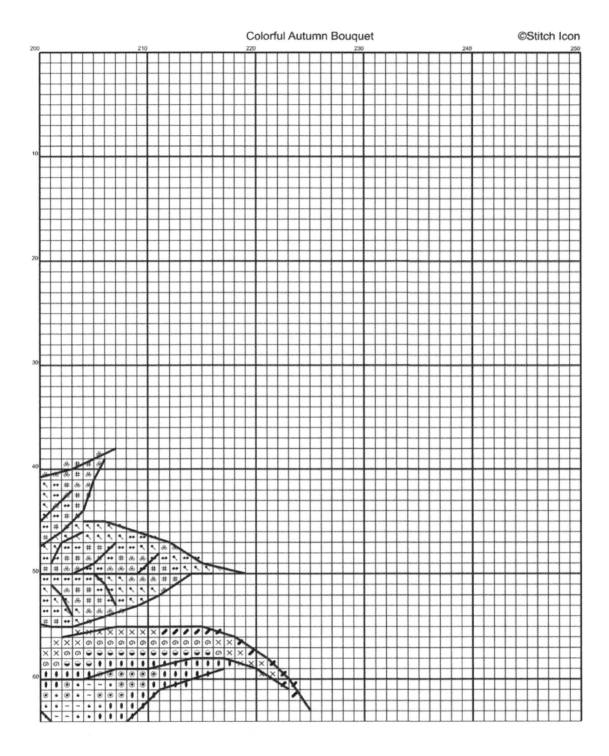

159

Colorful Autumn Bouquet   ©Stitch Icon

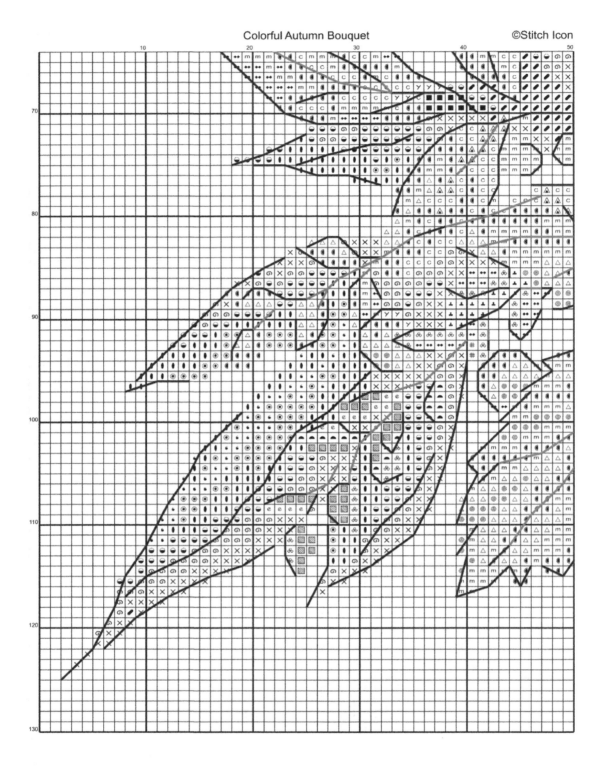

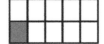

160

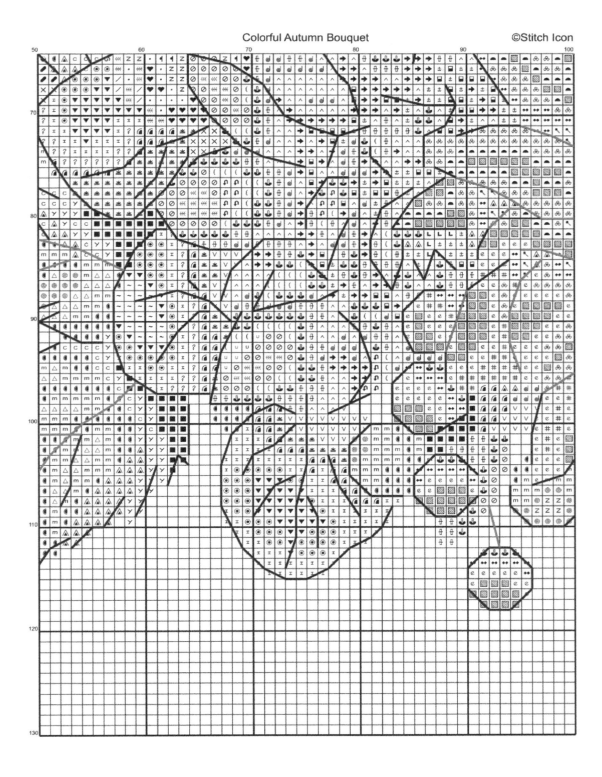

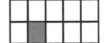

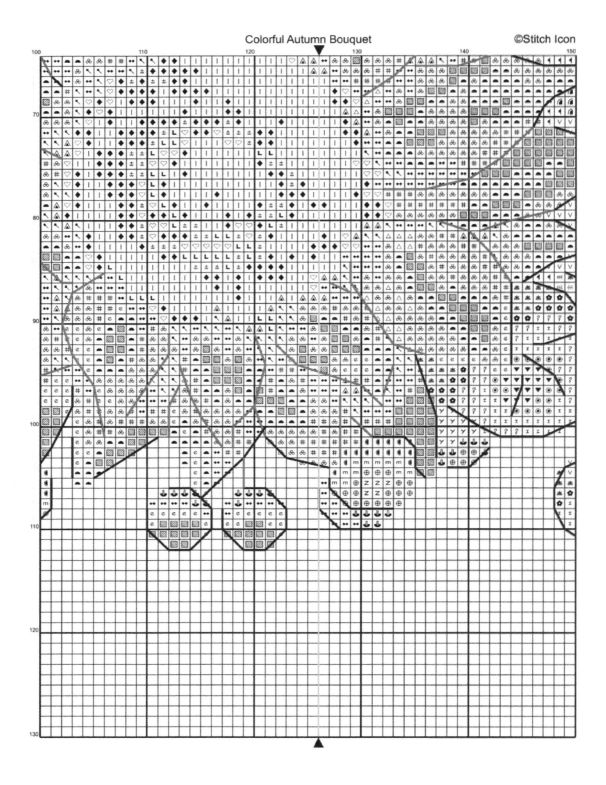

162

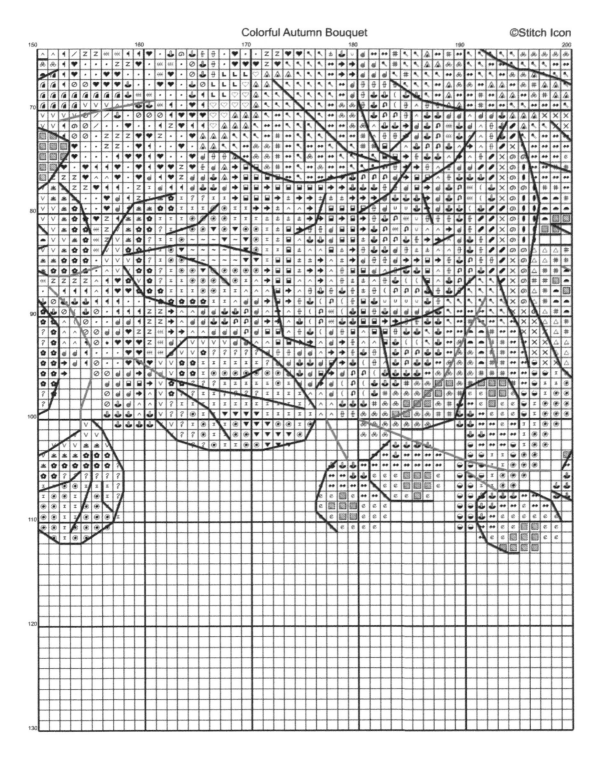

163

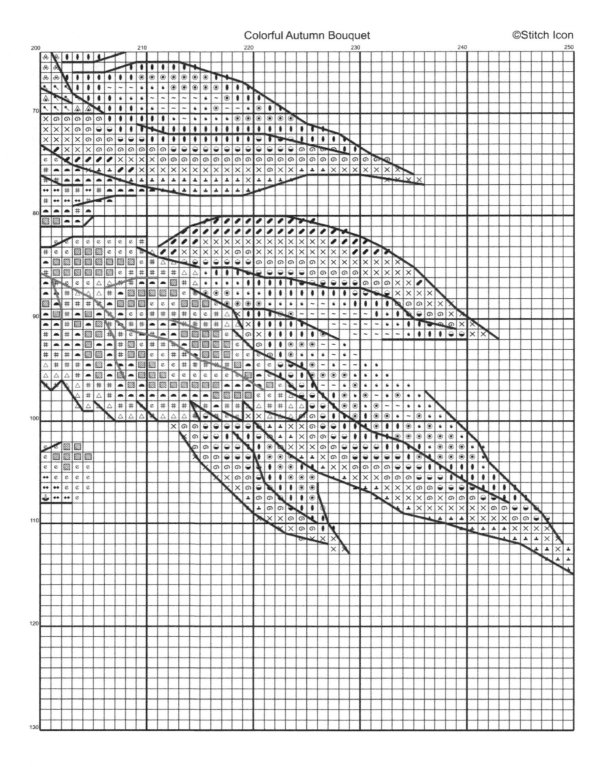

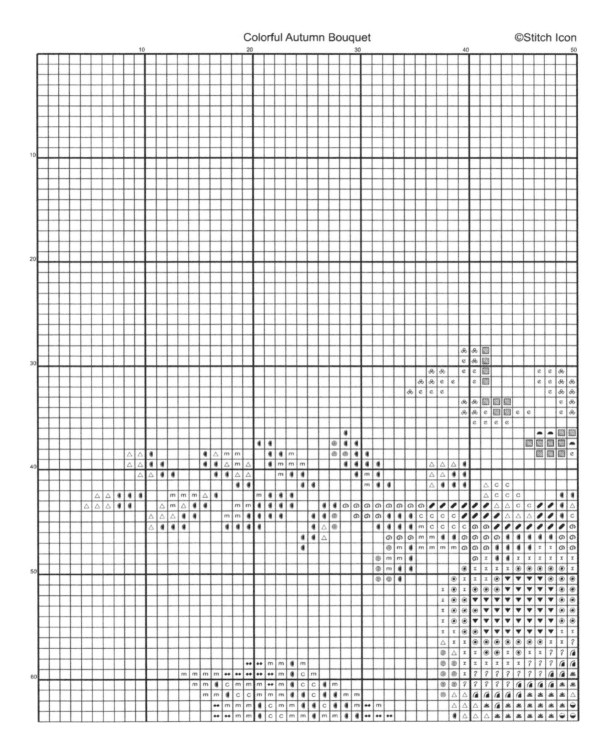

165

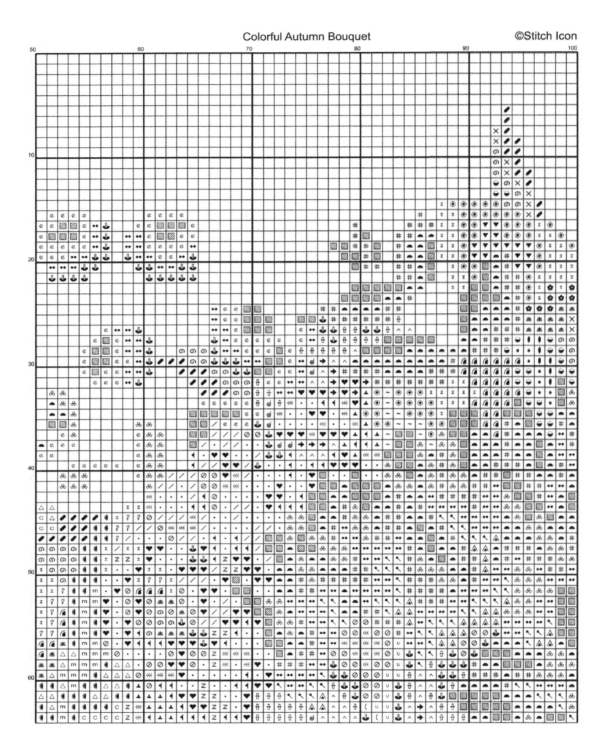

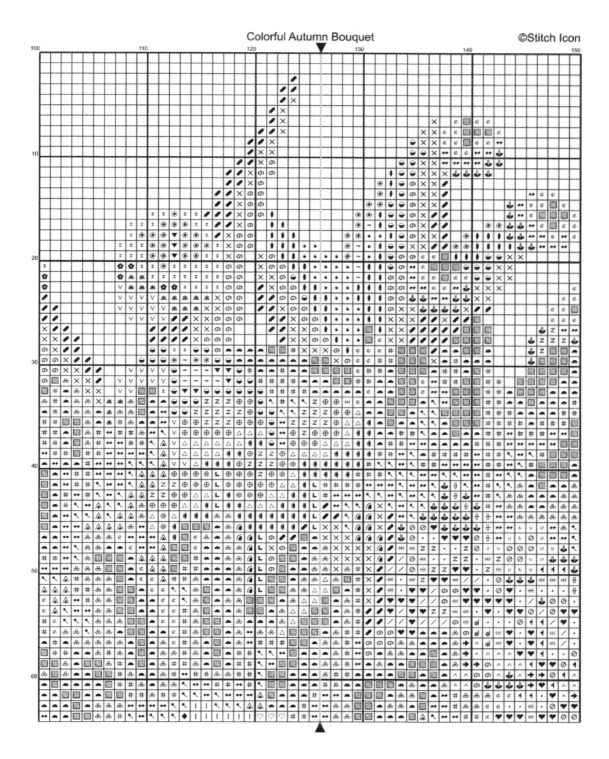

167

Colorful Autumn Bouquet

©Stitch Icon

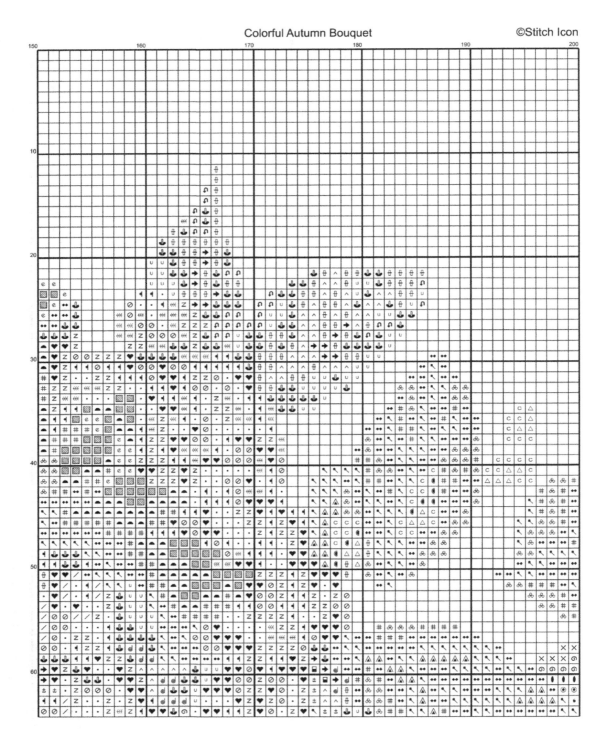

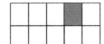

168

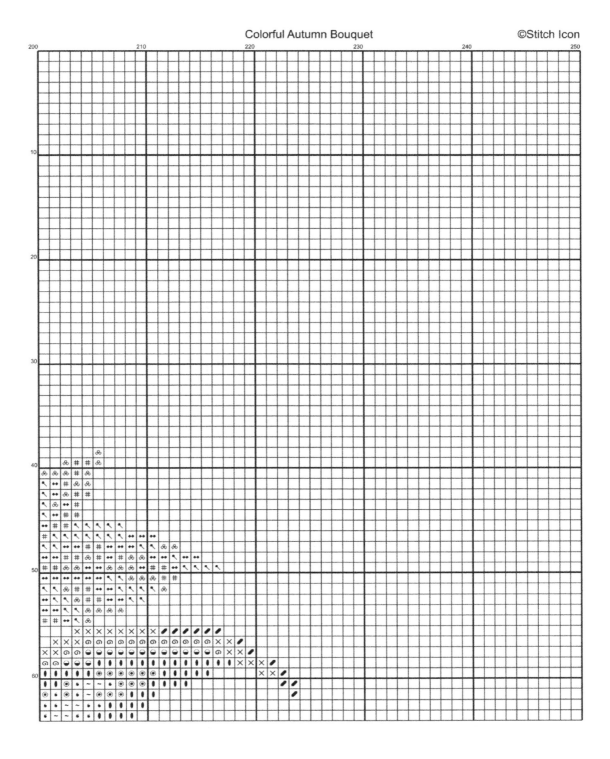

169

Colorful Autumn Bouquet

©Stitch Icon

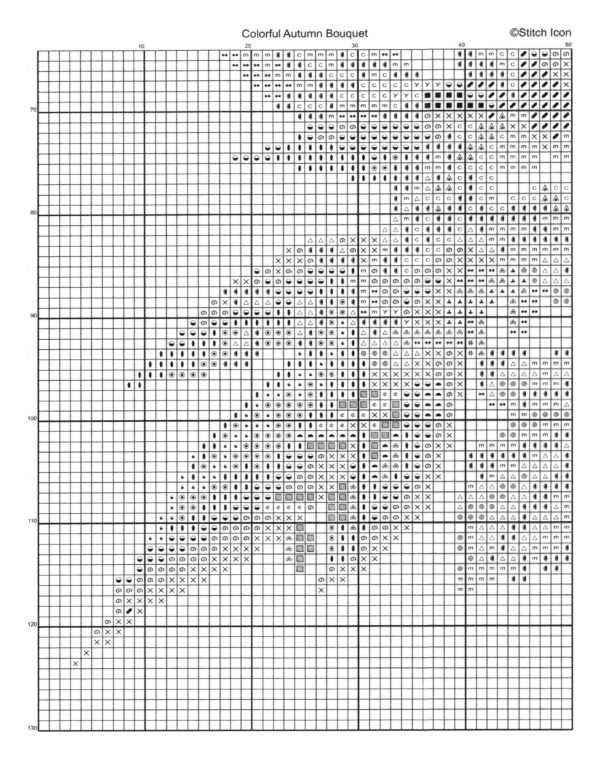

170

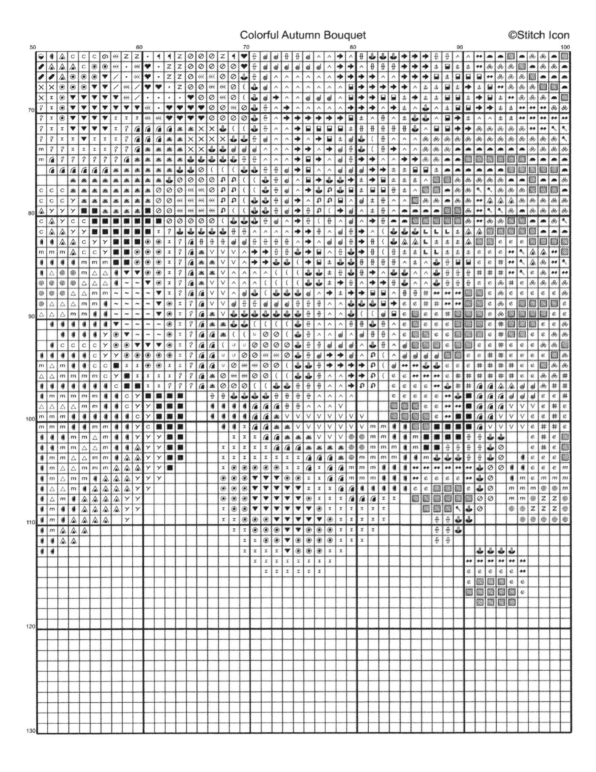

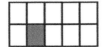

171

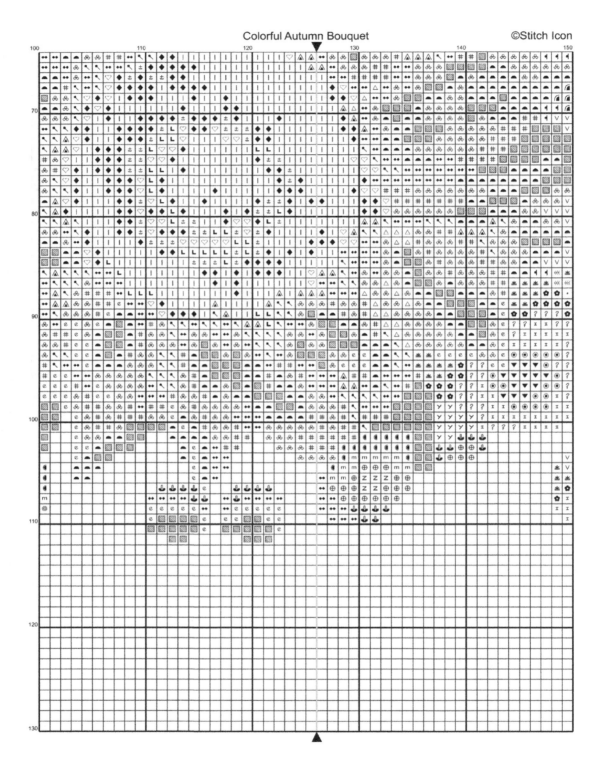

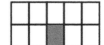

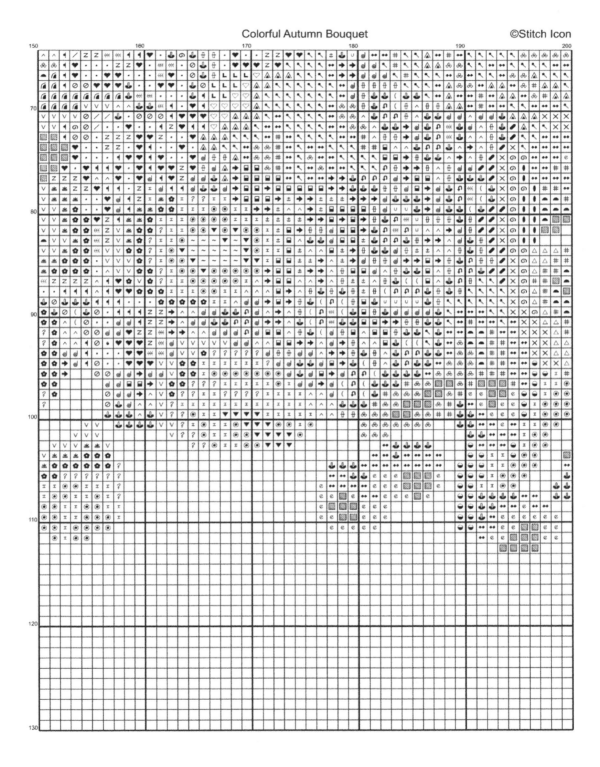

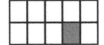

173

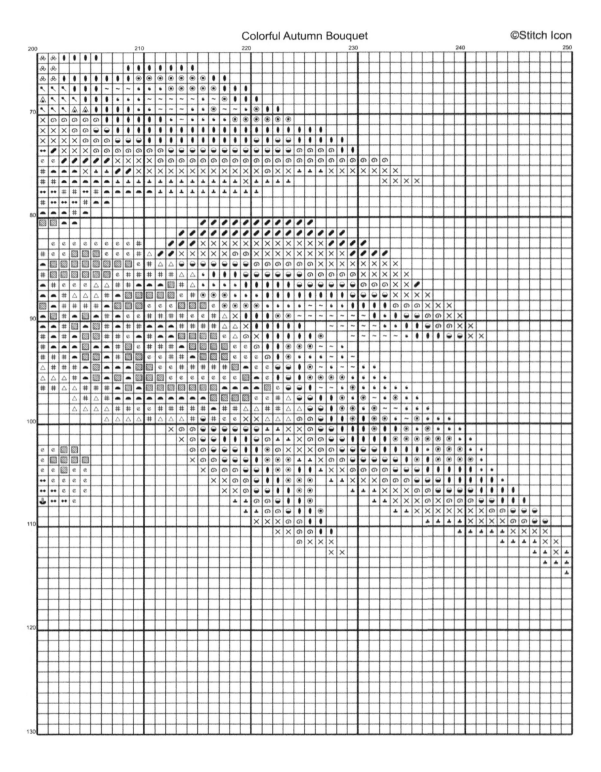

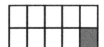

SPRING TREBLE CLEF

Overview
Palette: DMC
Colors: 29+2 blends
Stitches used: full cross stitch, backstitch
Fabric: 14 Aida
Chart Size: 89 x 114 Stitches
Finished Size: 162 x 201 mm or 6.36 x 8.14 inch

Melody Blooms: A Cross-Stitch Serenade

This design breaks the mold by celebrating the harmonious marriage of music and spring. Picture a cherry blossom tree, gracefully intertwined with the elegant curves of a treble clef. It's a visual symphony that will surely strike a chord with your music-loving pals.

With a clever selection of just 29 colors, this pattern proves that sometimes less is more. Each thread dances and weaves its way through the fabric, creating a melodic masterpiece that captures the essence of both spring's vibrancy and music's enchantment. It's like hitting all the right notes with a limited palette!

Measuring a petite 162 x 201 mm or 6.36 x 8.14 inches, this pattern is perfect for those who prefer short and sweet serenades. You'll be humming along with joy as you bring this delightful design to life. And when you present it to your music-loving friends, they'll be singing your praises!

So, grab your needle and thread, and let's create a cross-stitch composition that will make your heart sing. The "Spring Treble Clef" pattern is your ticket to a world where stitches and melodies entwine, leaving you with a harmonious masterpiece that will make you feel like a virtuoso of embroidery.

Prepare to be serenaded by the magic of cross-stitch as you embark on this melodic adventure. The stage is set, the notes are waiting to be stitched, and your creativity is the conductor. Get ready to witness the blooming of melodies as you weave your threads with laughter, joy, and a touch of musical mischief. Let the cross-stitch symphony begin!

Thread Length Table (DMC # / Length, meters)

DMC 15 - 0,54	DMC 601 - 0,39	DMC 816 - 0,29	DMC 3609 - 1,85
DMC 150 - 1,54	DMC 602 - 0,25	DMC 819 - 2,87	DMC 3687 - 0,31
DMC 153 - 0,42	DMC 603 - 0,25	DMC 3013 - 0,61	DMC 3688 - 0,21
DMC 154 - 3,78	DMC 644 - 0,25	DMC 3032 - 0,48	DMC 3689 - 0,28
DMC 223 - 0,73	DMC 747 - 0,92	DMC 3053 - 0,83	DMC 3727 - 0,97
DMC 316 - 0,28	DMC 814 - 1,19	DMC 3348 - 0,53	DMC 3731 - 0,77
DMC 326 - 0,28	DMC 815 - 1,38	DMC 3608 - 0,49	DMC 3756 - 2,22
			DMC 3865 - 1

Instructions and Symbol Key for Design "Spring Treble Clef"

Fabric:	**14** count
Stitches:	89 x 114
Colours:	DMC

Size: 6.36 x 8.14 inches or 16.15 x 20.68 cm

Use **2** strands of thread for cross stitch

Sym	No.		Sym	No.
≃	15		~	150
⬟	153		☐	154
●	223		⋘	316
▰	326		I	601
⊕	602		◓	603
◓	644		▫	747
Z	814		▨	815
✿	816		◓	819
⊥	3013		◖	3032
♥	3053		/	3348
♡	3608		▪	3609
⬇	3687		◮	3688
L	3689		?	3727
⬇	3731		)	3756
⟩	3865		◗	819 + 3609
◉	747 + 3756			

Backstitch

Use **1** strand of thread for backstitch

——————— DMC 154

Use 2 strands of thread for backstitch

——————— DMC 154

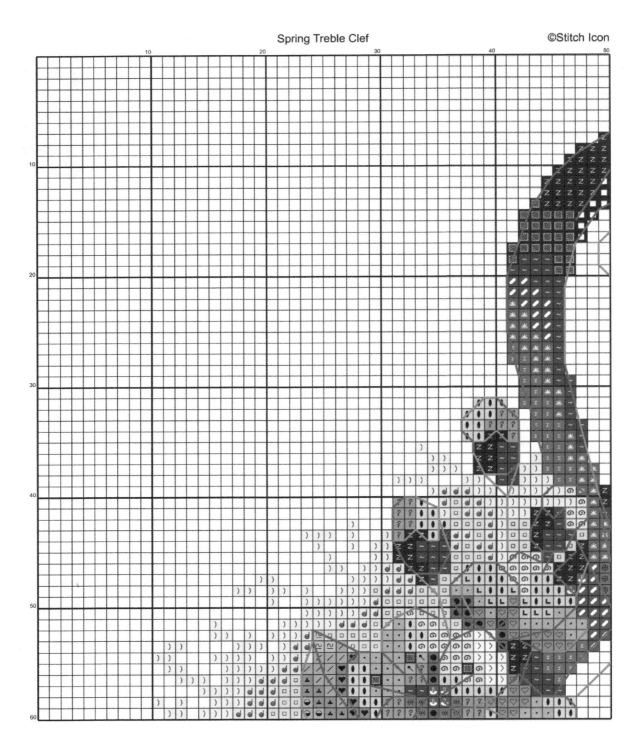

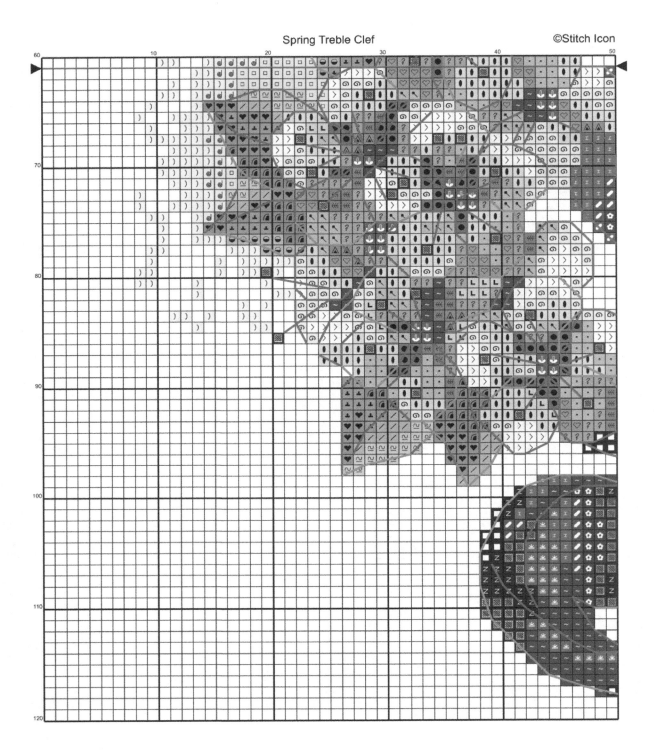

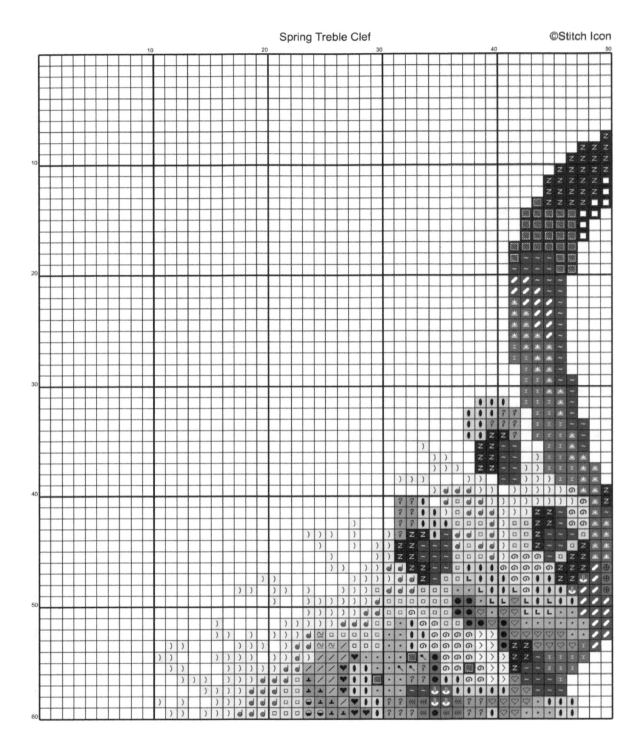

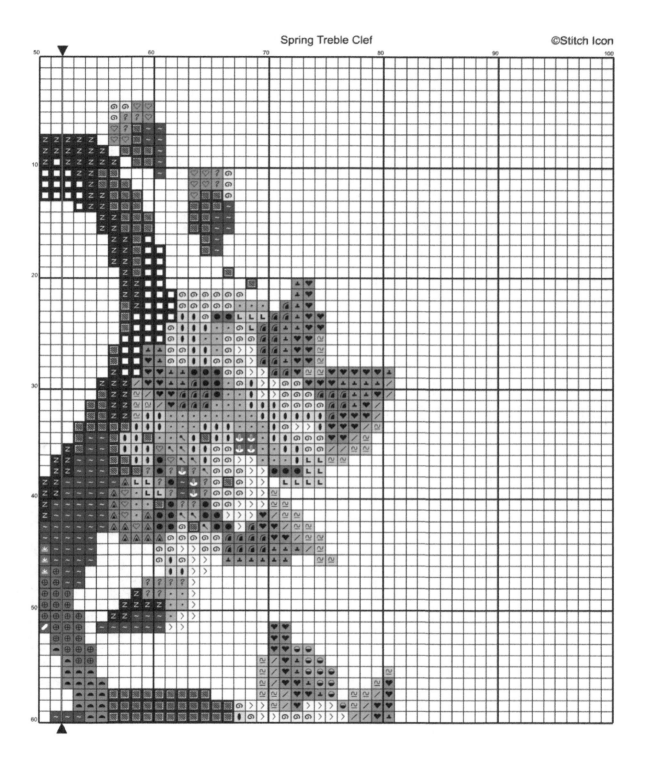

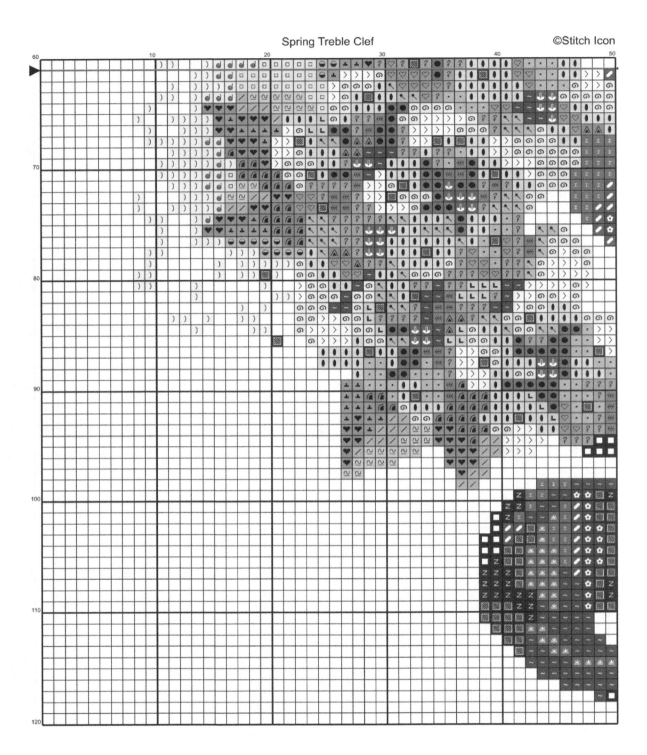

185

Instructions and Symbol Key for Design "Spring Treble Clef"

Fabric: **14** count

Stitches: 89 x 114   **Size:**   6.36 x 8.14 inches or 16.15 x 20.68 cm

Colours: DMC

Use **2** strands of thread for cross stitch

Sym	No.		Sym	No.
ℛ	15		~	150
↖	153		■	154
●	223		⫷	316
◗	326		ᴵ	601
⊕	602		◖	603
◓	644		□	747
Z	814		▨	815
✿	816		၅	819
⊥	3013		(a	3032
♥	3053		╱	3348
♡	3608		·	3609
⚓	3687		⚠	3688
L	3689		?	3727
⚓	3731		)	3756
〉	3865		❶	819 + 3609
⏧	747 + 3756			

Backstitch

Use **1** strand of thread for backstitch

———————   DMC 154

Use **2** strands of thread for backstitch

———————   DMC 154

Spring Treble Clef ©Stitch Icon

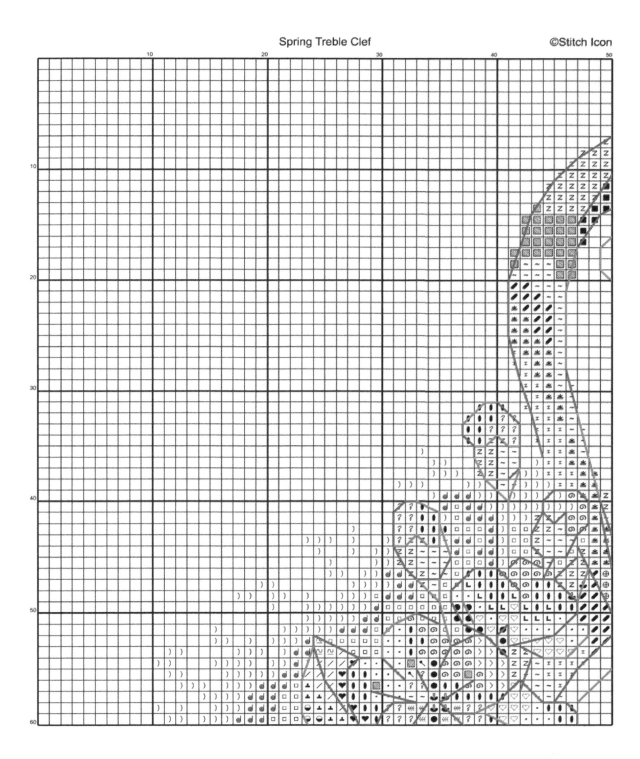

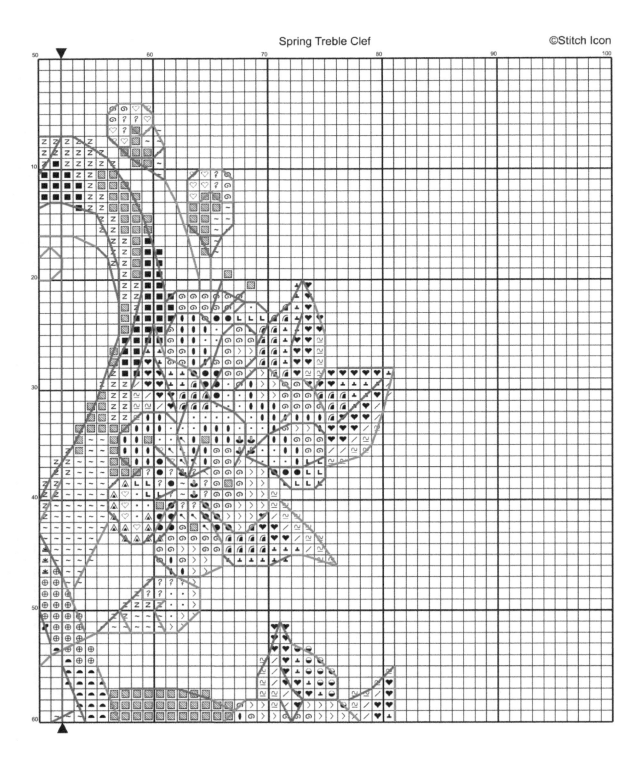

Spring Treble Clef

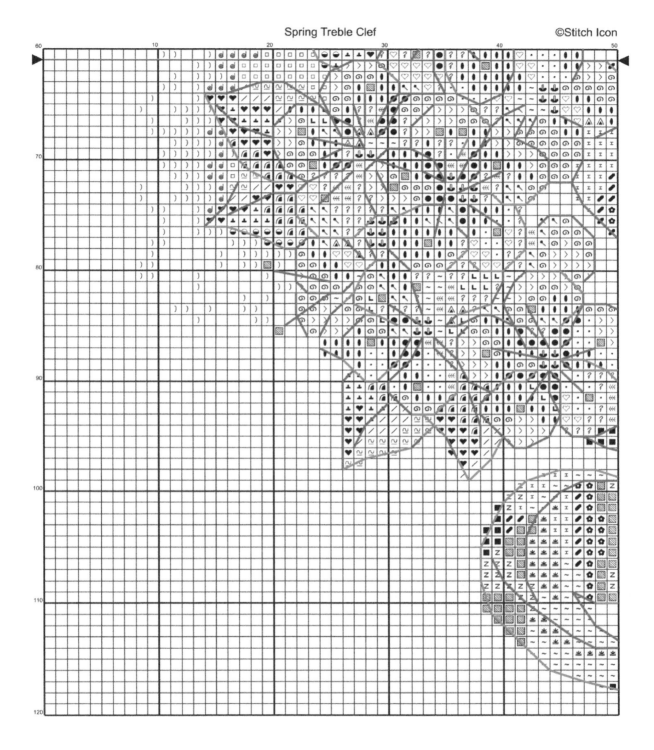

189

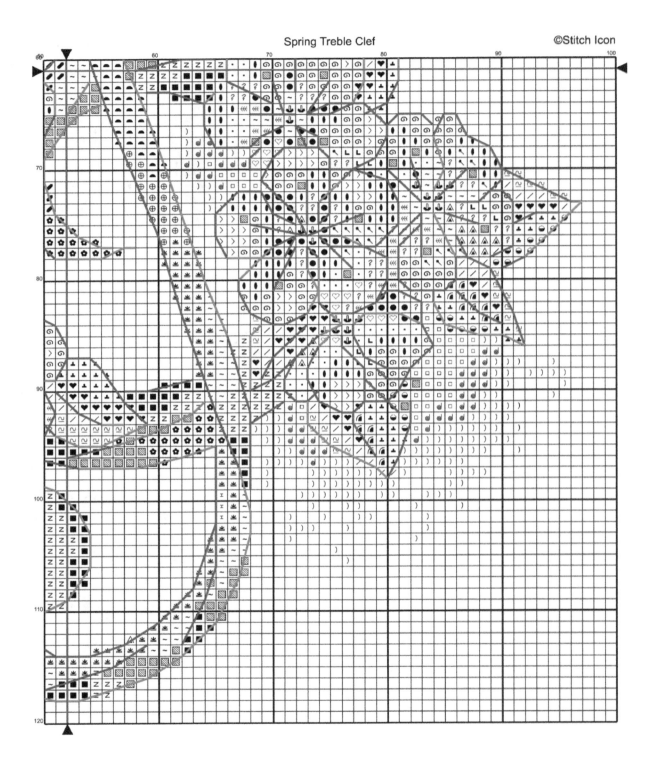

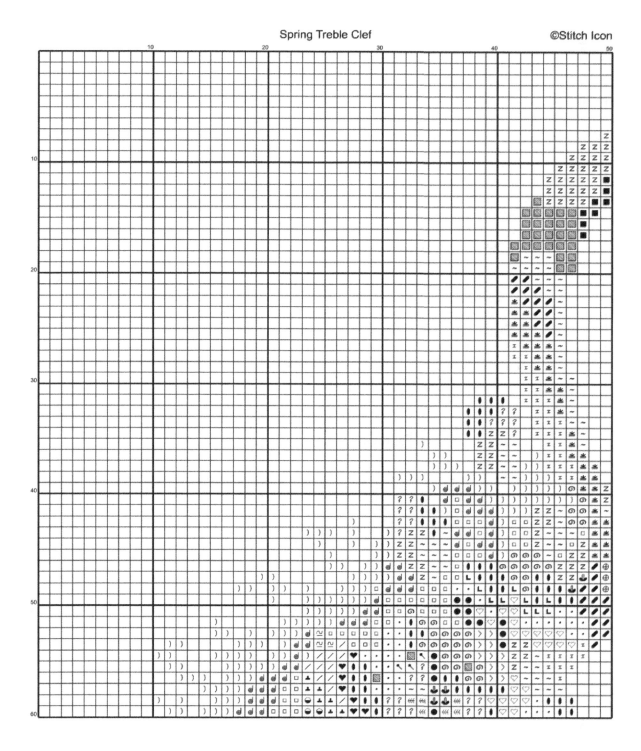

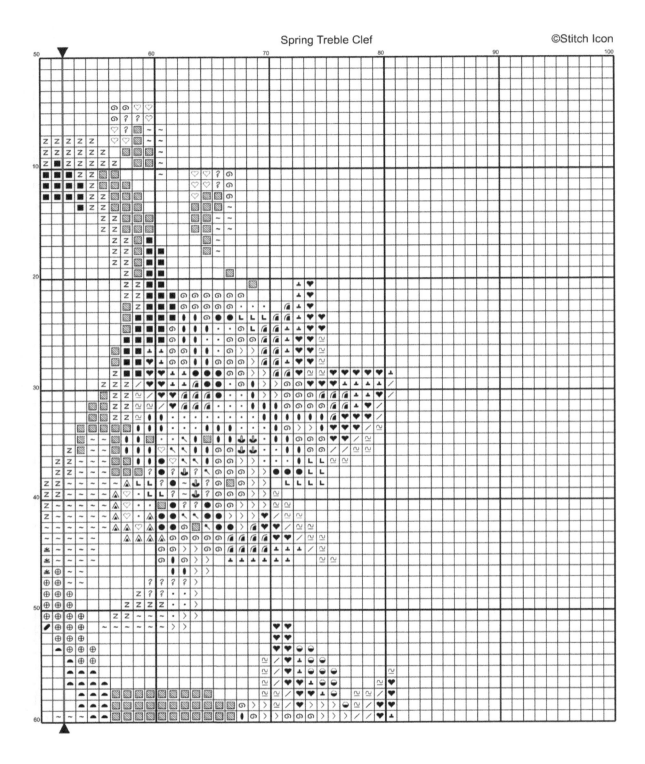

Spring Treble Clef

©Stitch Icon

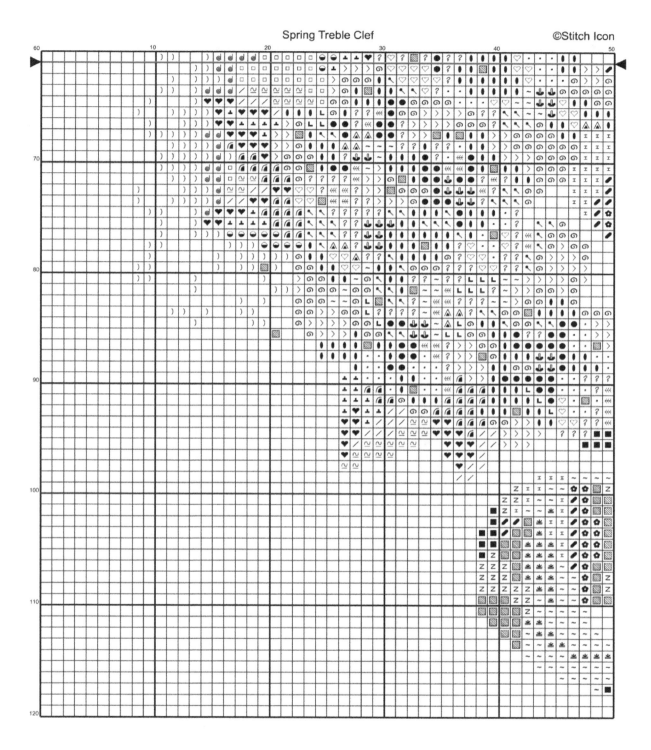

193

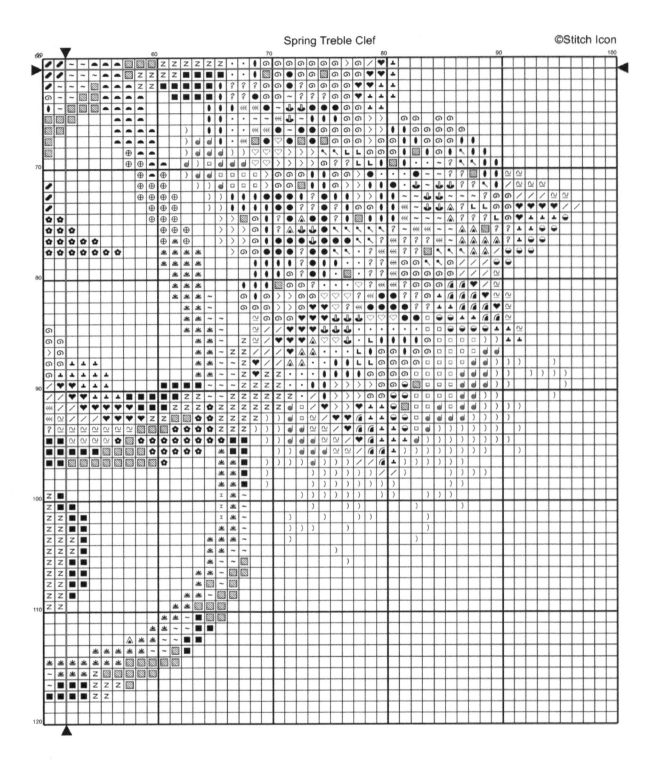

THANK YOU!

Thank you for choosing "Cross Stitch Pattern Book: Floral Patterns - Stitching through the Seasons." We hope that you enjoy stitching these beautiful floral patterns as much as we enjoyed creating them. Your satisfaction is our top priority, and we would greatly appreciate it if you could take a moment to leave a review and share your thoughts about the book.

Your feedback and reviews play a crucial role in helping us improve and create even better pattern collections in the future. Your honest opinions can help other stitching enthusiasts make informed decisions and discover the joy of creating with our patterns. Whether you loved the designs, found the instructions clear and easy to follow, or have any suggestions for improvement, we value every comment.

Leaving a review is simple and only takes a few minutes. Your support not only encourages us to continue creating quality patterns but also helps us reach more stitchers who can find delight in our designs.

We appreciate your support and look forward to hearing from you. Thank you for being a part of our stitching community and for helping us spread the joy of cross stitch through your reviews. Happy stitching!

Organize your threads like a pro with our floss organizer box and bring your designs to life with our wide selection of vibrant embroidery floss sets.
Shop now!

Amazon   Stitch Icon   Etsy

Made in the USA
Las Vegas, NV
10 September 2023

77355068R00109